MacArthur Came Back
A Little Girl's Encounter with War in the Philippines

MacArthur Came Back

❖

*A Little Girl's Encounter with War
in the Philippines*

By Leanne Blinzler Noe
with Barbara Noe Kennedy

Copyright © 2012, 2013, 2020 Leanne Blinzler Noe and Barbara Noe Kennedy. All rights reserved. No part of this book may be reproduced or transmitted in any form or by any means, electronic or mechanical, including photocopying, without permission in writing from Barbara Noe Kennedy, barbaranoekennedy@gmail.com

First edition with second round of revisions.

ISBN: 978-0-615-60296-7

Book design by Kay Hankins and Barbara Noe Kennedy. Cover design by Barbara Noe Kennedy.

Front cover photos: Top: MacArthur returns to Leyte, the Philippines (Department of Defense, Department of the Army, Office of Chief Signal Officer); bottom left: Leanne and Ginny dressed like little Igorots, Baguio, before the war (courtesy of Leanne B. Noe); bottom right: Former internees celebrate liberation in 1945 (Carl Mydans, Life Images).

Back cover photos: Left: Former roommates Connie Ford, Dorothy (Dot) Mullaney, and Leanne in front of their former classmate/prison in 2005; right: Soldiers during Battle of Manila, February 1945 (AP Photo).

Follow *MacArthur Came Back* **on Facebook.**

*To my Parents,
to the Brave who Rescued us,
and to my Family*

CONTENTS

	Map of the Philippine Islands	IX
	Map of the Pacific Theater in World War II	X
	Introduction	XI
1	Siskiyou County, California	1
2	Marinduque & Manila	13
3	Baguio	21
4	Escape to Manila	29
5	War	33
6	Santo Tomas Internment Camp	37
7	Liberation	59
8	Return to the U.S.A.	69
9	Settling into American Life	73
10	Return to the Philippines	75
11	Back to the U.S.A. for Good	79
	Appendix	83
	Acknowledgments	101

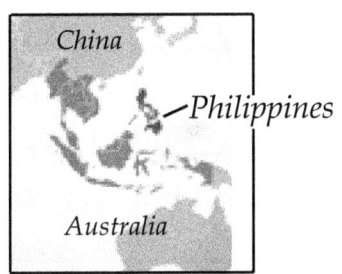

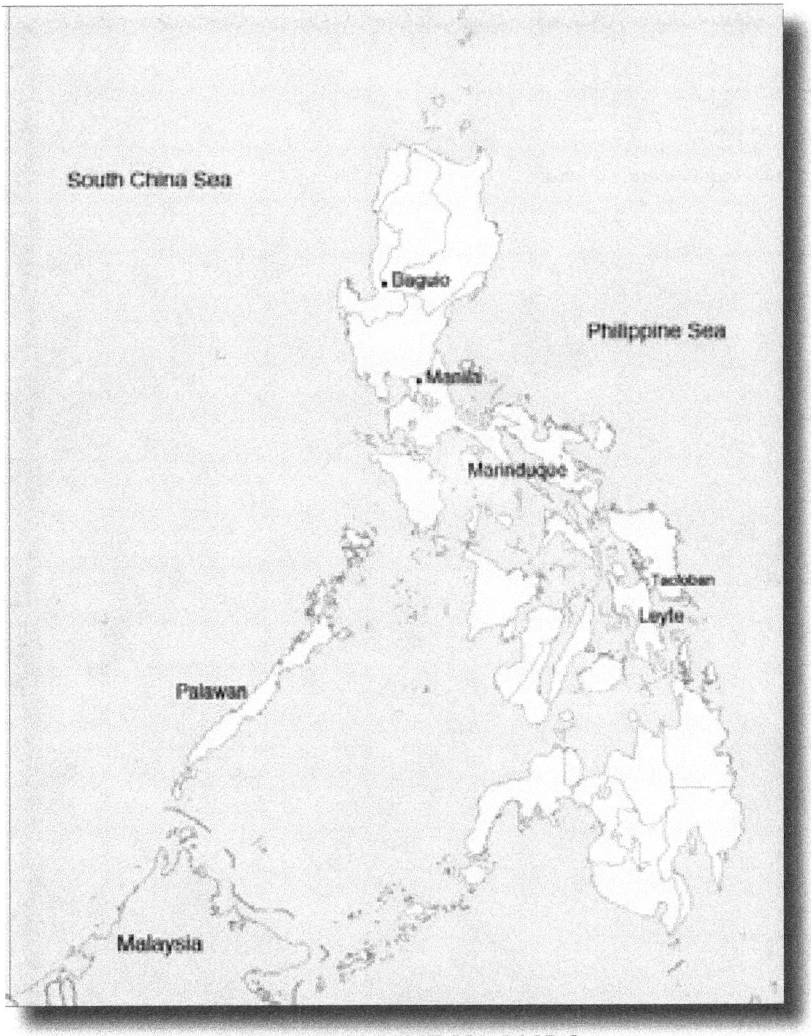

THE PHILIPPINE ISLANDS

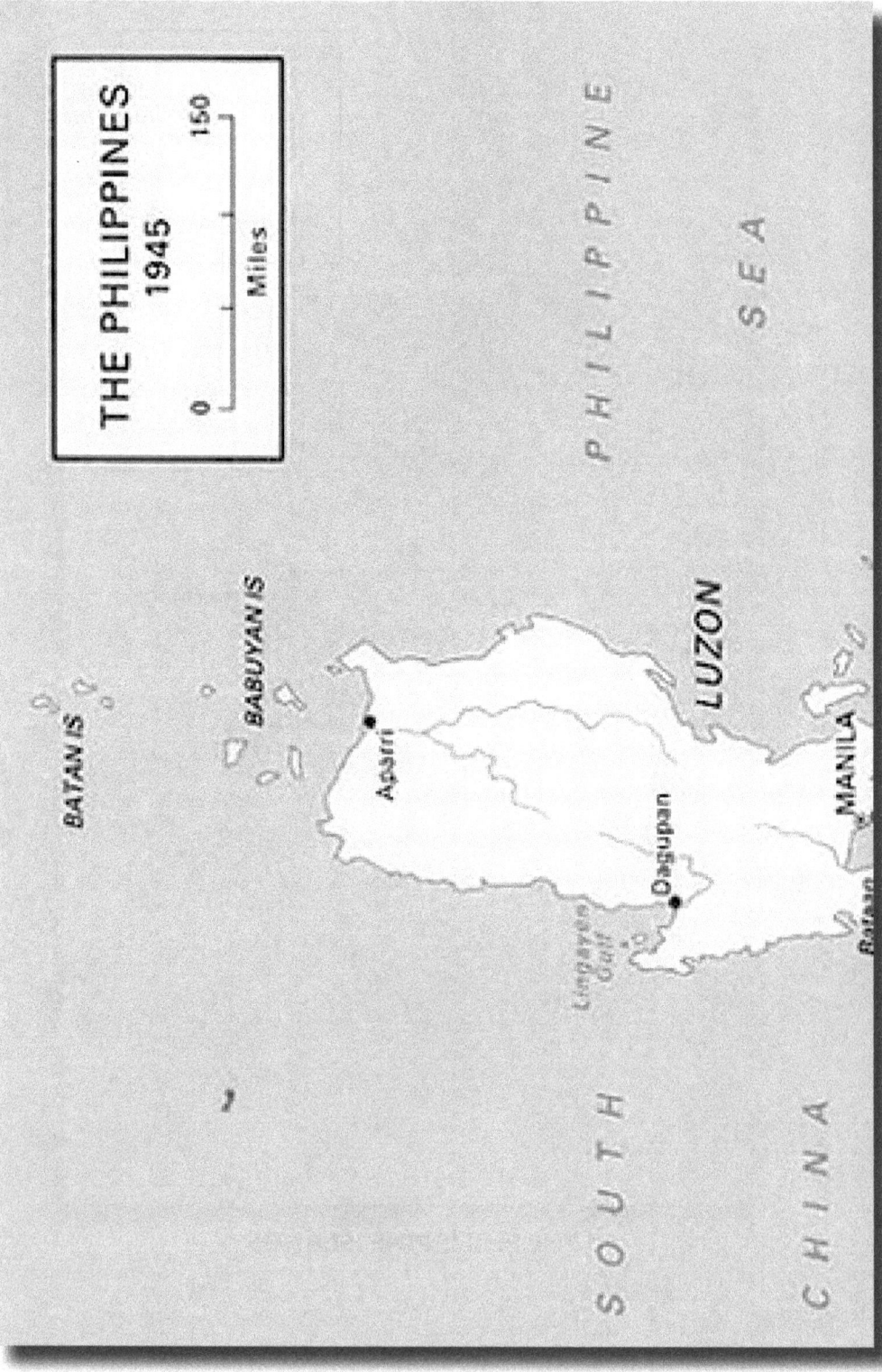

INTRODUCTION

GROWING UP IN THE *affluent city of Piedmont, California, across the bay from San Francisco, my two sisters and I had an all-American childhood. We played softball with family friends on the Fourth of July, went to church on Sundays, and every Christmas we rushed down to the blinking, angel-topped pine tree to unwrap piles of gifts. We went on vacations to Lake Tahoe and the Grand Canyon, collected $25 a month in allowance, and loved the days when our mother went grocery shopping — bringing home lemon yogurt, tortilla chips, and carob-covered peanuts.*

There were, of course, sibling bickering, parental disagreements, and the occasional yelling match. No family home would be bona fide without those. But in later years I realize that my mother worked overtime in creating a home, a stereotypical family life, because she had anything but that when she was young. It's probably something that she yearned for, given her atypical childhood.

As we were growing up, our everyday activities were sprinkled with random stories about my mother's girlhood memories of the Philippines — mentions of MacArthur and prison camp and roaming free in the hills of Baguio. My mother had a boar's hair toothbrush that she said she kept in the prison camp with her, and wooden statues of carabao and Igorots — natives who lived in northern Luzon, where her father worked at a gold mine. And then there's the one-inch piece of shrapnel — a ragged, sharp bit of metal — that had been shot into her jaw during the Battle of Manila, and which she keeps in her jewelry box to this day. To top it all off, she lost her mother at the age of three, so she and her sister were essentially raised by the nuns of Holy Ghost College & Convent in both Manila and Baguio.

It all didn't make too much sense to me, exactly how all these tales fit together. Especially the part about MacArthur. According to my history lessons at school, he was an extremely arrogant, difficult, controversial leader who ended up being forced to resign by Harry S. Truman. Yet I distinctly remember my mother telling me when I was a little girl that this man was her hero. As I grew older, I wanted to know more about what she meant, as well as the sequence of events of her childhood — more poignantly, how did she end up in a Japanese prison camp in Manila during World War II, and what was it like?

I've since enjoyed traveling twice with her to the Philippines, including one organized trip in 2005 with other civilian and military POWs, and she has spent hours with me talking about her memories and sharing letters written by her parents and other relatives and friends who were there. We have also attended several POW reunions, including the 75th anniversary of their Liberation in February 2020. She wanted to share all of this information with her family, her niece and nephew and cousins, and especially her grandchildren.

The result is this booklet, a chronological account of everything that happened to Leanne Blinzler and her sister, Ginny, and father and mother, Lee and Kay, from their earliest days in Siskiyou County, California, to their move to the Philippines, to the explosion of World War II all around them, as they became caught up in the Japanese quest for the Greater East Asia Co-Prosperity Sphere. And how Gen. Douglas MacArthur became entangled in their lives.

— Barbara Noe Kennedy (2020)

CHAPTER ONE

❖

Siskiyou County, California
Early 1930s

My mother's family in San Francisco dates back to the Gold Rush. Geraldine Bohen (Gran Edwards), my mother's mother, was born on Van Ness Avenue on the site of the Opera House in 1875. The belle of the '90s, she married Case Edwards, the son of a missionary Circuit Rider in Canada, in 1902. They moved to Manhattan for Case's business, where Rosemary (1904) and Geraldine (Jerry) Bohen (1906) were born, with Muriel (1908) and Katherine (Kay) Stuart (1910) and three boys, Case (1912), Robert Garrison (1918), and Wesley Harris (1919), following.

At Aunt Rosemary's wedding to Joe Hannan on April 9, 1928, some busybody revealed that Case was carrying on with someone else. Gran and Grandad later reconciled, but in the 1930s, she moved to San Francisco, living on Washington Street with Kay, Jerry, Case, Bob, and Wesley. It was during this time that Kay — my mother — somehow met Lee Edward Blinzler — my father; maybe through a friend of one of my mother's brothers, or a family acquaintance.

Kay told her family in August 1932 that she and Lee were going deer hunting around Yreka, in Siskiyou County, where he had relatives and worked at the Dewey Mine. Jerry divined that Kay may have different plans in mind. In a letter written to Rosemary (who was then living in Rye, New York) in that same August, she said:

"K looks too cute in the pink dress [you sent] and you couldn't have picked a better day to have all the things arrive. K had a phone call at midnight last night and Lee will arrive here at 4 p.m. She's going away with him next week to visit friends and go deer hunting in La Port, or maybe they will get married and go straight through to Yreka. If you ask me it's the latter from all the excitement we've noticed of late, she was

so pepped up this morning it was a scream and she's been deer hunting before. I think they'll just slip off and get married and then mother won't have a chance to try to plan a wedding. We can't afford one and K doesn't want it so I think she's right. They will drive up and stay with Lee's uncle until they're able to finish their own log cabin. ... When I left she was tearing around the house in it yelling 'Look at Mrs. Blinzler.'"

Jerry went on to say that Kay told Lee that she would rather have a Scotty dog than an engagement ring, because up in the mountains a dog would be company for her while he was at the mine and a diamond ring would only be a nuisance.

It turns out that Jerry was right. My mother and father eloped to Medford, Oregon, on August 27, 1932, then moved to Siskiyou County, a remote, mountainous realm in the northernmost part of California, near the Oregon border. The first three weeks of their married life, they lived with a *"whole bunch of people,"* presumably his Uncle Mush (Aloysius Fledderman), Aunt Marie, and their three daughters, in Yreka.

In those days, Yreka, with a population of some 2,500, was the center of the region's activity. Surrounded by chiseled granite mountains, it looked every bit a Western town (and still does!), with its false-fronted buildings along Main Street. Its newest buildings, however, gave a nod to current trends, including the one-story Montgomery Ward building on Broadway (1929), which would take 10 to 12 train carloads of merchandise to stock; the adjacent two-story, concrete Warrens Building (1930), which occupied an entire block and had offices upstairs and a bank and the post office downstairs; the Moorish-style Broadway Theatre (1930), lauded to be "equal to any theater in the larger cities and superior of any now in northern California or southern Oregon"; and the Ley Station, Yreka Fire Department (1930). The town had five auto dealers, three drug stores, a dry cleaners and laundry, furniture stores, gold buyers, six different grocery stores (including Safeway), two lumber stores, three hotels, four meat markets, six different places to shop for millinery goods, and 11 restaurants.

As soon as it could be arranged, Lee and Kay moved into a two-room cabin—we're guessing near the mine—paying $20 a month.

According to one of my mother's letters, they were *"thrilled skinny."* The cabin was furnished, and it had running water, gas, electric lights, and a very small plot garage. We know that while living at the cabin, they traveled to Yreka for meat and other supplies; the tiny town of Etna, where they had a P.O. box; and the even tinier town of Gazelle for the doctor.

There was much talk about wedding gifts in letters from relatives as word of their marriage took off. In a letter to Nannie (her maternal aunt) on September 15, 1932, Kay wrote: *"You wanted to know if I wanted linens or silver or a check. In my present circumstances, a check would be the most acceptable thing on earth. I have linen because Mother got that for me when I was engaged to John, and in a place of [illegible] the most simple things are needed. So I would rather buy dishes, glass-ware, and things like that."*

In a different letter, to Jerry, she continued to discuss wedding gift options:

"All of Mother's suggestions were fine but the Agnes Riley china. I have so little room for anything really nice up here and it would be a care about the green dishes. Are they the ones with the [illegible] gold. If so they are also too good. ... I do need pots & pans badly. Am still using a dishpan and coffee can. Could I have one egg beater? Tell Pink that a nice nest of bowls would be great and decidedly needed. Any of the other people can send what they want. Pewter is always nice, a pitcher, platters, vegetable dishes, salt cellars, and anything else that you can think of in that line. The blue vase and candle sticks would be lovely. ... If some-one down there can send me a book on silverware I can pick out the set that I want. If anyone should ask about that. I truly must start working now. My very best to you, hurry up and get well."

My mother did admit a bit of nostalgia to Nannie in her September 15 letter: *"At times like this it is so very hard to be far away from most of your family. We were all so close for so many years. Well perhaps one day I shall be able to persuade my fine husband to take Mrs. Lee E. Blinzler for a trip East. I certainly hope so. But we are most emphatically financially embarrassed."*

It's clear that my mother's sisters looked after her as best they could, from San Francisco and Rye, New York. Rosemary sent her a dress, to which she responded on September 8, 1932: *"I wore your dress and was properly admired; fortunately, it washes beautifully. After traveling through the hot valleys out here it needed it."*

She seemed to enjoy married life, though she worked hard. In a letter that she wrote to Jerry, she said: *"It seems the same routine every day. 6:00 breakfast, 12:00 lunch, and dinner a little more leisurely. I am becoming a famous stew cooker. Had curried rice for lunch yesterday and made it so strong that it fairly blew the top of our heads off. Lee didn't say a word and ate two helpings. I'll bet he felt miserable all afternoon. He is so darned appreciative that it is pathetic. I shall certainly have to be a big person to keep up with him."*

In a different letter to Jerry, she wrote: *"Lee comes home for lunch every day. We have to get up at six a.m. and it surely is cold. I almost froze to death this morning. They haven't put any wood in this place yet, so we can't do very much about it. But the days are truly hot. I bought $0.08 worth of stew meat this morning and the man almost threw it at me."*

Fun times were had as well. Though gas was expensive, and they had a hard time keeping the tank of their Ford full, she and Lee sometimes enjoyed evening jaunts in the surrounding pine-covered mountains. In one letter to her oldest sister, Rosemary, after such a drive she wrote: *"It surely is a beautiful night. Stars, moon, and all that goes with it. Warm enough to just wear a sleeveless dress. Quite perfect after foggy San Francisco."*

Every year a 49ers convention took place in Yreka, and the whole town came out for it. *"All the men have to wear red shirts and overhalls [sic] plus beards,"* Kay wrote to Jerry. *"Lee has quite the beard now and his mustache has assumed a very droopy appearance. They look awful. The women have to wear hoop skirts of that era. Marie raked one up for me from her mother's place. I look perfectly screwey – but if you don't do it they put you in jail right out in the middle of the street, and of course everyone stands and gawks, swell. The jail is on wheels and has a big sign denoting that it is such and bars. Looks like a cage and if you want to get out before 24 hrs. you have to pay $1.50. We only have $2.35 so if we are put in only one gets out and besides we won't eat. I guess we will look funny for the people."*

But there was always work to be done. She continued: *"This is *wash day ... so I had better start in. My wash is on the line but the place is filthy and all the shirts are ready to be ironed. Two miners* [probably my dad and his helper, who lived with us] *in the family sort of make a few shirts, etc."*

Gold Fever in Siskiyou County
A brief history

Siskiyou County's gold fever dates back nearly as far as that in the Sierra Nevada Gold Country. In March 1851, a mule train packer named Abraham Thompson, while traveling along the Siskiyou Trail from southern Oregon, stumbled upon gold near Black Gulch. Word got out, and by the next month, 2,000 miners were testing their luck at "Thompson's Dry Diggings." By June 1851, a gold-rush "boomtown" of tents, shanties, and a few rough cabins had sprung up. Several name changes occurred over the years, but today the city is called Yreka.

With 370 active gold mines working throughout the years, the region became the second most productive province in California, after the Sierra Nevada's Gold Country. Indeed, the area produced 1,773,000 ounces of gold between 1880 and 1959, with a large unrecorded amount produced between 1850 and 1880.

Discovered in the 1880s, Dewey Mine — my father's mine — is one of the noted quartz mines of Siskiyou County. It's located, according to the California State Mining Bureau Report XIV of the State Minerologist (1916), in Sec. 23, T. 42 N., R. 8 W, in the Gazelle mining district, about 12 miles southwest of the town of Gazelle in the Klamath Reserve. Owned by the Squaw Mining Company and comprising 100 acres, it sits at an elevation of 6,800 feet. The ore occurs in granodiorite, having a width of three feet; workings consist of a shaft 400 feet deep, a tunnel 920 feet in length, drifts, raises, and stopes, all comprising several thousand feet of development work. Equipment consisted of hoist, dwellings, and old ten stamp and Huntington Mills (poor condition) operated by steam and water power.

In its heyday, the Dewey was clearly one of the region's most legendary mines. In a 1966 article in the *Siskiyou Daily News*, J. O. McKinney wrote:

"In Siskiyou County's [1925] Economic Resources Survey there are 667 mineral deposits recorded. They range from agate to zirconite. But more than 500 of these are gold deposits. This is why anything that damages gold mining damages Siskiyou County. Gold has been a dominant mineral of the world for more than 19 centuries; it still dominates its field. That is why it is difficult for the layman to understand why the gold miner is not active here. A case to consider is The Dewey Mine. This mine is less than a dozen airline miles from the main line of the Southern Pacific Railway. From it to the railway at Gazelle is a downhill haul which would make for economic transportation. Ore there in seemingly unlimited quantities assays at $155 per ton. Had gold's worth spiraled as have the costs of other products today the ore would be near the fabulous price of $500 a ton. In years gone by, under supervision of John F. Boyle, one of the great mining men of the West, Dewey Mine paid handsomely. This storied mine is not all that is attractive in the location on China Mountain. The setting itself is romantic. A stream of mountain water rushes down through the forest which surrounds the old mine ruins. Even the mill tailings show ... gold not fully extracted under old methods. On China Mountain, too, are deposits of chrome, and asbestos; while on leased land under Bureau of Land Management herds of cattle grow fat on grass whose proximity to minerals makes it highly nutritious. Dewey Mine has always been closely tied to Siskiyou County and Yreka. Florian and Charles LeMay, now departed, were long-time working men there. Mrs. Rita Prather, of Montague, is the daughter of John F. Boyle, who brought the mine to its finest state of production. Rodney Gregg probably can relate many stories of the place, that while richer than many of King Solomon's mines is now standing in ruins. That is but one case of how Siskiyou County is now being handicapped by a monetary system we do not understand."

The same article featured a couple of "current" photos of the property, with several outbuildings still standing, but barely. Dewey Mine is said to have produced $900,000 total.

We weren't exactly sure until 2012 why my father was working at the mine, when we came across Fred Sater, whose family obtained the mine property in the sixties. His historical records show that Dewey Mine was most active between 1902 and 1906, with periods of operation in 1917–1919 and 1935–1942. In 1934

Frederick A. Wright of Oakland owned the mine, while my dad was the superintendent in charge of operations.

The work was hard on Dad, causing his arms to ache. "Every night when he gets to bed his arms go to sleep," Kay wrote to Jerry. "You can't bang them awake ... It is uncomfortable as heck" using the shovel so much. His uncle experienced the same ailment.

Before too long, it became clear that my mother was expecting. They moved to an apartment in San Francisco, at 2290 Green Street (though we're not sure if this was before or after the pregnancy). Rosemary sent her a box of baby clothes, which Kay was ecstatic to receive. On May 22, 1933, she wrote to Rosemary:

"Your box came this a.m. and I am still so thrilled I can't seem to come to earth and write any sense. My room still has the powder smell. You did it up so beautifully it was a pleasure to look at the box even without seeing all the wonderful things in it. The sweater on top was so nice and white, just adorable. Do thank Joe and Jerry for their cousin. Lee hopes desperately that the bow will have to come off the blue dress, and I don't even care. The idea of a baby boy or girl is quite enough for me. I am so darned thrilled that I can't wait. Your box made the idea seem very real. ... I have been unable to buy anything, let alone pink coats with elephants and all those beautiful handmade dresses. The way you have the diaper folded looks so much neater than any that I have ever seen. I have been practicing and am very slow. But by the time that little B comes, if I don't wear the diaper out first, I should be quite good at it. I am so dumb about such things and they all mean so much to the comfort of the child."

On June 18, 1933, I was born. At first I was called Anne, but with a strong resemblance to my dad (chip off the old block), the name Lee was added—for Leanne. At some point in the next year, our little family moved back to the Yreka area.

My mother wrote Rosemary on February 12, 1934: *"Lee just adores Leanne and she him. She can say 'Dayce' now and 'hey dere' with the famous 'By By' to complete her 7 months vocabulary. Frankly, I don't* know how on earth I ever had such a smart child. She isn't at all like me in any way and Lee is darned smart. Fortunate for my children that one of us is."

My mother folded me into her daily routine. In spring 1934, she wrote: "There is snow still but it is warm and beautiful all of the time. Leanne is out on the side porch all morning after her bath until 2:00 or so. Then she sits up out there for a few more hours in the p.m. unless we go for a sleigh ride some place. She loves it up here and just thrives."

Even in the middle of the woods, my mother enjoyed nesting, making our house into a home. She wrote Rosemary:

"I am painting still or yet. This place was all dull grey and I have been making the living room ivory. Started cream but couldn't get enough paint. So changed … we look so clean and nice. Finished our room in cream and green. Then Leanne's room is perfect. The walls are turquoise blue and the woodwork pink. I made a stencil fuzzy little white lamb, to go around the wall, with a pink ribbon at a rakish angle. Then I have pink and blue flowered voile for curtains. Her crib is pink with a blue and pink spread. I like the results very much. The closet has a pink door with a lamb with a blue ribbon. I certainly love to fix up a place particularly as the company supplied the material. Lee was laughing the other day, thinking what some tough miner will say one day if such ever has to occupy that room.

I am enclosing a snap of Leanne taken at 7 months and one week, on the side porch. She looks awfully old for her age, doesn't she? But she is darling and so much company. I never knew that an infant child could be so little trouble and so darned good."

In the same letter to Rosemary, she revealed that another little one was due. "[Leanne] isn't quite paid for yet and we are expecting a little brother in July or early August. I am awfully glad to have them so close of an age. They should be very companionable and lots of fun for us. … Mother doesn't know about my expectations so please see that the news isn't relayed. I will tell her at a much later date."

In June 1934, my mother went to the doctor's office in Gazelle, where she learned that *"little B"* was expected to arrive early. She sent an urgent letter to Rosemary, asking that a layette be sent sooner than requested. The pregnancy seemed to have affected her health slightly. On June 18, 1934 — my first birthday — she went to a dentist office in Yreka to have a third tooth extracted. *"This pregnancy has certainly wrecked my mouth completely,"* she wrote to Rosemary. *"Had it all put in order when I first knew but still my teeth die. Just had one pulled on Saturday and Sunday another one blew up. Speaking of hags, I surely look just like one, but hope to have six pivots put in after the big event."*

My birthday went by somewhat unnoticed — my fourth tooth was coming in, so I was experiencing tooth pain. Henry the Japanese boy, who was paid room and board to help my mother with washing, ironing, and cooking (at this time my father's helper and his *"sulky, independent, and dirty"* 12-year-old daughter were living with us), gave me a cute brush and comb set plus a high chair tray. My father's brother, Uncle Urb, gave me a little gold and white necklace with a pendant sporting a small diamond and "Leanne" written on the back — *"awfully dainty and pretty,"* wrote my mother.

Virginia (Ginny) indeed arrived early, on July 1, 1934. Her birth is recorded on July 5 in the *Siskiyou News* of Yreka.

The next letter we have is dated October 21, 1935, when our mother wrote Rosemary that the dresses she sent arrived — *"The green one is awfully smart and fits very nicely. Is it supposed to have a belt? I thought of using a grosgrain if it hasn't one as it is large through the waist and hangs too much away but if you have a belt for it I can send the money for you to ship it. I am awfully glad to have them all and do appreciate your thought."*

She added that Lee went to San Francisco for some kind of business *"with the desired results, so we are getting along again after rather a strained month. Mining certainly has its ups and downs, principally downs. We haven't starved yet so I shouldn't complain."*

She may have been alluding to the fact that since the United States had gone off the gold standard in 1933, gold mining had become a very tough business. Possibly hearing about the mining opportunities in the Philippine gold mines through friends from the Colorado School of Mines, where he had studied, he decided to head to the Far East in 1936 to see for himself what fortunes were to be had.

Mother-Daughter Visit to Yreka, 2009

Note from Barbara Noe, Leanne's daughter

Mom and I visited the Yreka area in September 2009 and tried to locate the Dewey Mine. Not many people knew about it, except for the son of a tourist bureau employee who hunts in the backcountry. He told us to take a road out of Stewart Springs, which is different from what I had researched by topo map and Google Earth. I had figured we had to go south of Gazelle on Gazelle-Callahan Road, then turn left onto Dewey Mine Road. Mom and I began to have trepidation about finding it.

At the Siskiyou County Museum, we told the woman working behind the desk about our quest. She pulled out books and maps, but we didn't really find anything. In the museum itself we found a picture of the mine in its heyday (before my grandfather's time), ten men hanging out in front of a wooden shaft, with big logs lying in front.

Driving south on Route 3, we stopped at a forest service office in Fort Jones to ask if they knew anything about the Dewey Mine. A helpful ranger spent some time helping us check a map and locate the mine, exactly where I had thought it was. He said it was a dirt road, and we'd need a four-wheel drive.

We had lunch in Etna, where Kay and Lee had a P.O. box. The little town hasn't changed much since their time—one street with Western facades, the highlight being Scott Valley Drug, in business since 1902. Its soda fountain was brought across the plains via prairie schooner.

From Etna, we followed Gazelle-Callahan Road through the mining ghost town of Callahan and up a steep mountain. At its crest I spotted what I believe to be Dewey Mine Road, off to the right. But it was dirt (we were in a normal car), and if the mine was indeed located along the road, it was at least 4 miles in. It's still wild, beautiful country, all pines and clear, rushing streams and cattle-dotted valleys.

Back in Yreka, in a sun-scorched plot overlooking the jagged mountains at St. Joseph Catholic Cemetery, we found the tombstones of various relatives on my grandfather's side: Aloysius George Fledderman (1888-1977); Appalonia Pontzer (1849-1933); August Fledderman (1848-

1940); Herman Joseph Fledderman (1881-1962); Marie Opal Fledderman (1900-1980); Richard Fledderman (1885-1927); Christina Fledderman (Tina) (1887-1986); and Rose Lauer (1878-1965). We also saw a historic butcher's shop (which had recently gone out of business), and probably was the one that Kay mentions in her letters. Here, too, stands the Elks Lodge, which, in the days when Kay and Lee lived in the area, was a theater. Established in 1904, the theater featured a bandstand built over the sidewalk for outdoor music and a speaker's forum. See p. 94 for a published travel story about this adventure.

CHAPTER TWO

❖

Marinduque & Manila
1936-1939

THE PHILIPPINES HAS LONG BEEN FABLED for its gold. According to a *Newsweek* article dated April 26, 2008, Spanish conquistadors, when they first arrived in the Islands, noticed that the natives were bedecked in gold ornaments from head to foot. It's reported that all those centuries ago, the Filipinos were so knowledgeable about gold that even children could accurately determine the purity of gold alloys. The locals also had a sophisticated vocabulary for gold and indigenous goldsmithing techniques, as recorded in the 16th-century Tagalog-language dictionary collated by Pedro de San Buenaventura.

In the fall of 1936, Lee Blinzler headed to Marinduque, a heart-shaped island province south of Luzon floating in a turquoise blue sea. It's a beautiful land of rolling hills, pretty valleys, and plummeting seaside cliffs, speckled with coconut, banana, and rice plantations — and gold mines. As soon as he was settled, he sent for our mother, Ginny, and me to join him.

Three years old at the time, I apparently did not enjoy the ship's journey across the Pacific. *"For Leanne's sake,"* our mother later wrote to Rosemary, on January 12, 1937, *"I hope she doesn't [remember] as I know her idea of the sea would be one place of much nausea."*

The only memory I have is being in my mother's arms, with festive streamers being tossed from the ship at one of the ports.

Arriving in the Philippines on October 29, 1936, our family moved into a nipa hut, a native house made of bamboo with a thatched roof, set on stilts with chickens scampering beneath. We had running cold water, *"but must heat it on the stove,"* our mother wrote. Two puppies kept Ginny and me amused.

Our mother had help with the housework; she seemed especially taken by the *lavenderas* — washerwomen. She wrote to Rosemary:

"They usually put the clothes on a rock in the river and squat & swatting with a wooden paddle until most of the clothes are swat to pieces but the dirt comes out. I must pay my two 12 pesos or $6.00 a month because they can't pound my clothes. The poor things asked such a high price because I am a very particular person. Feature two washerwomen for $3.00 each. They have huge irons in which burning charcoal is put. And then again squat on their heels and iron away. It surprises me to see how much they accomplish with nothing modern. My camera just came and I am going to try to get a picture of them with the wet wash on their heads coming from the river to hang it. They use their feet quite aptly as we use our hands."

The Blinzlers were among the few Caucasians on the island, our mother wrote. "It is very different, to say the least. The language of the natives in Manila and also Marinduque is Tagalog, and I find it very difficult to learn. There is no grammar and a word can mean many things depending on the use. Not so simple."

She went on to say that "there was an enormous mining boom going on in the Philippines, helped along by cheap labor. A man will work an 8-hour shift in the mine for .75 centavos or 37 1/2 cents. They live on rice and fish so their expenses are nothing. They go to sleep when it's dark and get up when it's light, ergo no light. And should there be a fiesta they hollow out a bamboo and pour coconut oil in which makes a fine blaze and costs nothing."

1936 was a big election year, pitting Franklin D. Roosevelt (D) against Alf Landon (R), but our mother seemed far removed from American politics: "The native has few wants and the white man is well paid so from a personal standpoint we didn't care who was president," she wrote to Rosemary. "The strike is slowly putting us on chicken, rice, and various native foods as canned goods are scarce. We have enough for six months for the babies, so I am not going to worry about that. We were also for Landon."

Presumably, the strike she was referring to was the one that began in San Francisco on October 29, 1936, in which every facet of maritime transportation, including firemen, engineers, mates, cooks, sailors, and longshoremen, stopped work up and down the West Coast for 99 days. It's interesting to note that Alf Landon was supported by the ship owners; perhaps my parents' support of him tied in directly to the delivery of food and other goods to our remote outpost in the Philippines.

Our first Philippine Christmas — 1936 — was *"very grand,"* according to a letter our mother wrote. *"They each [Leanne and Ginny] got a car to ride in, doll carriages, table and chairs, and a lot of junk. Poor babies were absolutely exhausted but very pleased at the end of the day."*

Our mother and father did not exchange gifts; they devoted all their resources to Ginny and me. Tinsel and balloons decorated the nipa hut throughout, and a small tree was imported. It looked like a fairyland and *"both of the babies were very impressed."*

The locals helped make the day special by playing Dad's school song from Berkeley, and they had cock fights in between the music.

As of January 1937, our little family finally seemed to be enjoying the promise of economic stability. *"It is a very nice sensation to know,"* our mother wrote in her January 12 letter to Rosemary, *"we are climbing out of debt and in a year's time should be saving a bit. Four years of poverty operations and babies isn't easy but we do feel that 1937 will be good for a change. It so far is interesting."*

In January we moved from the nipa hut into a real house, with three bedrooms. On February 23, 1937, our mother wrote to her mother-in-law, Granny Blinzler:

"We have a lovely house and I have quite a few natives doing my work, which I adore as housework never held any charms. Natives are so cheap and eat only rice and fish so it is very possible to live nicely. Our house has three bedrooms, bath, kitchen, huge sala or living & dining room combined. We have sun-porchy furniture: very good looking. The furniture is brown and the upholstery brown and yellow. Our floor has no rug but is highly polished. The whole place is very cool and airy feeling. I like it a lot."

My sister and I also seemed to like our new home. Our mother wrote: *"The babies each have a swing and sand box, two pups, and quite a few toys. They are both perfect huskies. Virginia is positively fat and awfully saucy but very cute. Leanne is darling and such a pleasure.*

Her manners are perfect. We gave their horse away as he was quite mean. I tried him a few times and wasn't at all pleased. They are too young, I think."

Sadly, sometime in April 1937, our mother passed away *"suddenly and peacefully."* Not much is revealed in the letters that we have, but she died from tuberculosis. Clearly she was far from any hospital that might have cared for her. How did she contract it? We don't know, but can surmise that living in harsh conditions in Northern California, and undergoing a breached birth with Ginny, left her susceptible.

In a letter to his mother, Dad expressed how *"lonesome"* he felt, and he said what a *"real pal"* she had been and *"it did not seem true"* that she was gone. At first Ginny and I stayed with the Delahuntys in Baguio, but then our father placed us in Holy Ghost College in Manila, where a German order of nuns ran a school.

The next letter we have is from our dad to Rosemary, undated, from Santa Cruz, Marinduque. Rosemary had obviously heard about the tragedy, and Dad thanked her for her sympathies. *"The untimely passing of such a wonderful person really makes one wonder what life is all about,"* he wrote. He assured her that Ginny and I were getting along fine. *"Their youth makes them amenable to change more readily than if they were a year or two older."*

He said that it hurt him terribly to place us into the convent, but reassured Rosemary that *"the results have been very gratifying."* He said that he would like to take a trip to the States with the children to meet the family, and possibly enter us into a good school. *"Such plans, however,"* he wrote, *"will not be carried out for several years."*

In a later letter to Rosemary, dated August 9, 1937, our dad said that Ginny and I were doing fine. *"They are growing fast and seem to thrive encouragingly. They have outgrown the dresses they took to the convent with them. I had planned to send to the States for clothing, but was pleasantly surprised to learn that beautiful little dresses can be made at the convent, and at a low cost. The Mothers and Sisters take much pride in caring for the children, since they are the youngest there."*

He went on to describe Holy Ghost College in Manila, on Mendiola Street (now called Holy Spirit College): *"It is a large place* and has instruction from kindergarten through college. The specialties are music and the social sciences. The boarders, however, are much in the minority in enrollment. The children get good attention.... and most of the children are from the better families of the Islands. The sisters are mostly Europeans, but odd as it may seem, the Mother Superior is an American – a highly cultured and able person. One of the Sisters in constant touch is a former German baroness. I am glad to have them get an early training under such circumstances as it should make them tolerant of people of all nationalities later, instead of being taught to 'hate the British,' as I was. They talk much now, and their accents are precious."

At Holy Ghost, Ginny and I clung closely to each other, frightened at first by the nuns in their black and white habits. Ginny hadn't been baptized yet. I believe we went next door to San Beda and one of the priests baptized her there. We were placed in kindergarten, as there was no preschool. I had two years of it, and Ginny had three. We wore tan and white uniforms with sailor collars. I remember building scenes in a sandbox table, including small figurines, and singing a song about a family. I also recall both my sister and me dressing up several times as angels for a nun's jubilee celebration, or perhaps for Christmas. I also remember coming downstairs on Christmas and finding a tree and presents for us in the sewing room.

One night I was taken from bed and carried outside—I think it was an earthquake. According to *Time* magazine, indeed, a huge earthquake struck in August 1937; it was Manila's worst earthquake since 1882.

Among the nuns, Mother Superior was very pretty. Sister Edelwina was Holy Ghost's first directress, from 1920 to the war years; during her tenure she expanded the school, opening the high school and the collegiate courses. Sister Witburga was born in 1895, a big, loving woman who sometimes gave us treats. She seemed to be in charge of the kitchen. (A story is recounted about Sister Witburga in the *Philippine Daily Inquirer,* dated June 4, 2008. She is remembered for the German bread and chocolate fudge that "became culinary treasures of the school." When Sister Witburga lay dying, she was asked to leave her German bread recipe, which she declined, saying: "I have accomplished so little. Let my recipes die with me. They are nothing.") Sister Carencha was a big, stern first-grade teacher. Once she reported Ginny and me to Mother Superior because we brought snails we had collected in the large garden to the kitchen to be cooked. The nuns would give us one of the long pins that held their veils to their heads to pull the cooked snails out. We enjoyed eating them.

Out back a stone grotto stood by a pretty pond, graced by a blue-and-white statue of Mary. Sometimes Ginny and I visited with our dad here, when he had a chance to get away from his work at the mine.

Aunts Tina and Phil's Visit
Notes from Aunt Tina Fledderman's travel diary

On September 17, 1937, Aunts Tina and Phil—our dad's aunt and sister— arrived in Manila. Dad met their ship, the *Meerkerk,* on a launch and helped them through customs, presumably dropping their luggage at the Manila Hotel. According to Aunt Tina's diary, they picked us up at Holy Ghost, took us for a drive and then to their hotel, where they gave us dresses and books before returning us to the school. After a late night in town they left early the next morning by train and boat for Santa Cruz, Marinduque. There they drove to the mine, where they stayed for two weeks.

They met some of Dad's friends. Aunt Tina writes in her diary about driving to a Philippine movie in the capital city of Boac, 25 miles from the mine. They also went by truck and boat to see huge pythons worshipped by locals. On the way they passed colorful marine gardens of coral and tropical fish. They visited the mine buildings, hiked, saw a cockfight, played bridge and poker, and visited with friends while Dad worked.

They returned to Manila, calling on Ginny and me at Holy Ghost, taking us out for an afternoon of visiting, with white bread and butter a special treat. Boarding a bus, Aunt Tina and Aunt Phil went on to Baguio, where Dad's college friends, the Delahuntys, met them and showed them around the market, the gold mine where they lived, and the St. Louis School, where silver filigree jewelry was made.

In November 1939, milling operations in Marinduque stopped when prices on lead and zinc decreased. Dad found work in a gold mine outside the mountain retreat of Baguio, in northern Luzon—and we kids, me set to enter first grade, went with him. He lived at the mine, while Ginny and I resided at Holy Ghost Hill, the summer home of the Holy Ghost sisters.

CHAPTER THREE

Baguio

1939-1941

PERCHED AT 5,000 FEET, surrounded by precipitous mountains, Baguio in northern Luzon has long been celebrated for its pine trees, white gardenias, and strawberries—the year-round temperature hovers at 70 to 75 degrees Fahrenheit, drawing Manila residents especially during the long, hot, humid summers. When the Americans came to Baguio after Spain ceded the Philippines to the United States in 1898, they fell immediately in love with the rugged setting, ideal for retreats from the sweltering lowlands. They constructed Kennon Road through Bued River Canyon, an amazing engineering feat. The military built a large base here, Camp John Hay, where U.S. servicemen flocked for rest and recreation.

But there was one thing that the region was most famous for—its minerals and natural resources: silver, copper, pyrite, limestone, and especially gold. The Igorots who had lived in the region for centuries mined gold for their own pleasure. When Spanish colonists arrived in the 19th century, they snatched off their gold earrings and beat them into crucifixes. The opening of Kennon Road ushered in a mining boom in the 1930s, so that by 1939 fourteen mines were operating, including Balatoc, where our father had been employed.

On "moving day," in 1939, Ginny and I took the train from Manila with several of the Holy Ghost sisters. We transferred to a bus for the final stretch up into the mountains. Within time, we felt Baguio's cool climate.

We were the only two boarders at Holy Ghost Hill, the nuns' summer retreat. School took place at a picnic table beneath nearby pine trees or in a small room; we were soon joined by several Spanish boys who lived nearby (including Francisco Xavier Aberastori). It never seemed like work to study. Though one difficult aspect was that, being left-handed, I had to learn to write with the right hand. I sat for hours copying nursery rhymes until I finally mastered it.

I remember boiling mint tea leaves and cooking rice in a clay pot given to us by a priest. Monday was washday, when, just before sunrise, a fire was lit outside under a very large metal pot that was filled with cold water. The flickering light would be reflected into our upstairs bedroom.

I felt very close to nature in this gorgeous setting, with my pet snail in a shoebox, a bird that I was able to hold for a little while before it flew off, and hikes in the neighboring forest (one of the sisters was collecting and studying colorful spiders!). We had two dogs, Nora, the mother, and her puppy, Prince, born in a den by the side of a winding dirt path on the property. We also had a cat, Mimi, that I once watched getting the better of a snake. Another time I was taking the two goats for a walk when the gardener startled them; the goats dragged me down a hilly path covered with slippery pine needles and I had to let go. Sometimes I collected the chickens' eggs, and I would let one blind chicken eat to its heart's content in the large feed box. An artistic nun once painted a picture of me feeding the chickens on the shell of an egg.

We took dance lessons in town. And once we were in a program where we danced the Highland Fling. Heidi, a German girl, came over to play at least once. We visited Baguio Country Club for Santa visits and Easter egg hunts.

Our dad came to visit from the mine on weekends (mainly Sundays), when we'd do something fine—swim at Asin Hot Springs, or go down to the ocean at Miramonte, with stops in the barrios along the way to watch a cock fight or pose in front of a carabao. Friends usually went with us.

Other times, he'd take us to Burnham Park in Baguio—with its roller-skating rink, canvas-covered swings, a lake for boating, and ponies for riding. We girls preferred the pony rides. The native horses were small compared to horses back in the States. Filipino men would show their horses, trying to prove his horse was the best. He'd walk under it, show us how gentle the horse was. After we made our choice, the man walked the horse around with us on it; he'd let go when we asked him to. A field of grass, with little hills, added to the excitement.

Some weekends, Ginny and I hopped the Balatoc Mine's bus at Brent School, at the end of the nuns' driveway, to see Dad at the mine. There, we walked across the bridge to the Mess Hall, where he lived with fellow miners—in addition to the cook's pet monkey. I remember the big breakfasts. Dad had a Sears catalog that we looked through for shoes and clothes. I thought the motorscooters looked like fun.

On September 8, 1940, I celebrated my First Communion at the Holy Ghost Hill chapel. It was a beautiful sunny day filled with happiness. The nuns sewed my white dress complete with its drawstring purse in matching white fabric. Dad, however, thought the dress too long. We celebrated at the Baguio Country Club.

As world politics heated up, there was talk of war, and the expectancy that it might start at some point, as well as the fact that the Philippines could be a strategic Japanese objective. Indeed, as early as the 1930s, the Japanese had sent thousands of spies to see how strong the U.S. force was in the Philippines. A Japanese man once stopped by the convent to sell goods tied up in a large piece of cloth and tossed over his shoulders. Later, there was talk about whether he was a spy.

Everyone, however, believed that the U.S. government would protect its citizens in the Philippines, and we would be safe. Looking back, of course, this was not true.

General Douglas MacArthur had an unusually close relationship with the Philippines. His father, General Arthur MacArthur, had helped defeat the Spanish in the Philippines and went on to serve as its military governor. Upon graduating from West Point in 1903, through the years Douglas MacArthur went on to hold various jobs in the Philippines, including his first assignment, as a young lieutenant with the Army Corps of Engineers. After MacArthur finished his tour as Chief of Staff in 1935, he elected not to retire and, instead, with Franklin Roosevelt's approval, accepted President Manuel Quezon's offer to supervise the creation of a Philippine Army. MacArthur took on the task of transitioning the inadequately trained Filipino soldiers into a large, well-trained army of civilians led by professional soldiers with the intention that, by 1946, the year that the Philippines would gain independence from the United States, "the nation would have a trained military force of forty divisions, comprising about 400,000 men."

In typical MacArthur style, the general insisted on being given housing in Manila comparable to Malacañang Palace. A penthouse suite was thus renovated for him at the stately Manila Hotel with the most luxurious of amenities, including air-conditioning, a private swimming pool, and a view of Manila Bay. The next few years were probably the happiest in his life. He met and fell in love with Jean Marie Faircloth, with whom he had a son, Arthur IV.

But then, in July 1941, with war with Japan imminent, Roosevelt recalled MacArthur to active duty in the U.S. Army as Major General, and named him Commander of the U.S. Armed Forces in the Far East. By October 1941, MacArthur had 135,000 troops, 227 assorted fighters, bombers, and reconnaissance aircraft, and he claimed the Philippines as the "key or base point of the U.S. defense line."

Washington's plan for the Philippines in the event of war, part of a larger strategy called War Plan Orange, was to implicitly recognize its loss; the plan called to withhold assistance to the Philippines and other U.S. outposts in the western Pacific in favor of protecting the Panama Canal and bases in California, with the intention of the Pacific Fleet coming to the rescue at a later point in time. MacArthur, however, convinced Washington to agree to an active defense plan, called Rainbow-5, which permitted the defense of the entire Philippines in the case of a Japanese invasion. More military personnel began to arrive, including officers to train the Filipinos. MacArthur firmly believed that the Japanese would not attack before April 1942, to the point of having no strategy to defend the islands should an attack come earlier. He stockpiled goods, but even as his staff plotted to defend Manila from attack, the circulating joke was about "fighting a war and hangover at the same time."

Meantime, while arrangements throughout 1941 were being made to ship military and diplomatic dependents back home, and American businessmen and their families began leaving other Asian countries in a mass exodus, civilians living in the Philippines were advised to stay. Correspondence declassified 60 years after the war gives a clearer picture of the situation.

On October 9, 1940, Francis B. Sayre, High Commissioner to the Philippines, wrote to Cordel Hull, U.S. Secretary of State: *"...the State Department has instructed our Far Eastern consulates to advise Americans living in the Japanese Empire, China, Hong Kong, and French Indochina to return to the United States. So far as the Philippines are concerned ... there is no reason for anxiety ... Manila is one of the safest places in the Far East today."*

On January 7, 1941, Sayre wrote Hull again: *"I am of the opinion that at the proper time the Department should consider whether American civilians are to be evacuated either from Manila area or the Philippines..."*

The State Department added its two cents in a memo dated March 17, 1941, which essentially clinched the Americans' fate: *"If the Philippines are threatened by an enemy power, are we going to tell and assist Americans there to depart, and thus subject ourselves to the accusation by the Filipinos ... that we are fleeing from our own soil and leaving our wards ... to face the danger alone? ... we should tell the High Commissioner that we do not contemplate an evacuation of Americans from the Philippines ..."*

After that, American civilians had little chance to leave the Philippines, despite the fact that the prospect of war was becoming inevitable. On June 21, 1941, Congressional Legislation (22 U.S.C. 228-229) formally prohibited Americans from leaving: *"U.S. citizens were barred from departing from or entering any territory of the United States without a valid Passport."* Since all American citizens had been asked to turn in their passports on September 9, 1939, no one could leave if they wanted to. At this time, 7,300 Americans were stuck in the island archipelago, anxiously watching how world events would affect them.

The Japanese attacked Honolulu on December 7, 1941. The Philippines learned about the strike—and the U.S. declaration of war on Japan— just eight hours after the event, about 3:30 a.m. on December 8 Philippines time. Records show that at that time, Washington sent a cable directing MacArthur to execute the Rainbow-5 war plan immediately (which mandated that the Far East Air Force stationed in the Philippines should attack any Japanese forces and installations within range). MacArthur did not do this. Nor did he relay the message to his commander of the Far East Air Force, Maj. Gen. Lewis Brereton. He did not put his command on a full war footing.

Some say he was stunned, frozen at hearing the devastating news. Others speculate that he held off an attack in deference to Philippines President Manuel Quezon, who hoped that the Japanese would not attack the Philippines if the Philippines did not attack first. Quezon later stated that he told Maj. Gen. Dwight Eisenhower in Washington in 1942: "When the Japanese attacked Pearl Harbor, MacArthur was convinced for some strange reason that the Philippines would remain neutral and would not be attacked by the Japanese."

The exact chain of the military events that transpired that December 8 is murky, but Brereton is said to have requested permission twice to bomb Formosa (Taiwan) airfields—and he was twice denied. An attack finally was approved at 11 a.m. on that day, but it was deferred until a reconnaissance mission was completed.

Meantime, Brereton, knowing the Japanese often attacked at dawn, feared that the grounded planes at Clark Airfield—the headquarters for the Far East Air Force—would be caught and destroyed, so he had ordered his pilots to take off and circle the airfield. When no dawn attack transpired, due to a heavy fog, Brereton ordered the planes down at Clark to refuel and await their next orders.

Between 8:30 and 9 a.m., Japanese planes entered Philippine air space. They struck Baguio first, bombing the Military Circle (the Main Gate of Camp John Hay), inflicting the first casualties of war in the Philippines.

A warning of an imminent attack sent to Clark and Iba Airfields, both on Luzon Island, was never received. A phone call didn't get through to the proper command, and a radio warning failed. At about 12:30 p.m., the fighter pilots at Clark, who had come down from patrolling to eat lunch and refuel, had no idea that Japanese airplanes—108 bombers escorted by 88 fighters—were
en route. Imagine the delight of the Japanese pilots who came across 35 brand-new B-17 "Flying Fortressess" jets on the ground, lined wingtip to wingtip, fully armed, unmanned, the easiest target in the world. In one fell swoop the Japanese demolished half the Far East Air Force, including 22 of the B-17s, 56 fighters, and 30 miscellaneous aircraft—an attack considered as devastating as Pearl Harbor. After the bombing, the Japanese strafed the field, making sure that little remained. Eighty men were killed, and more than 150 wounded.

At Iba, the fighters were also attacked, but they managed to avoid the strafing attacks that had devastated Clark.

The next day, December 9, the Japanese forces hit Nichols Field, Cavite, and Davao, on the island of Mindinao, where a large colony of Japanese had been waiting for this moment— all part of a huge assault against the Philippines, Malaya, and Netherlands East Indies. Sometimes as many as 150 Zeros would accompany the Japanese bombers, making it difficult
for American fighter pilots to fight back. By December 10, U.S. forces had only 22 P-40s and eight P-35s left in the Philippines. On this same day, Japanese ground troops landed in the north at Aparri and Vigan, accompanied by the whirring of high-flying aircrafts, and MacArthur ordered that the remaining U.S. fighters be used mostly for observation. The Japanese on the ground converged toward Lingayen Gulf.

MacArthur radioed Roosevelt, calmly stating: "The military is on the alert and every possible defense measure is being undertaken. My message is one of serenity and confidence."

❖ ❖ ❖

Unaware of how the world had just changed, knowing it was a Holy Day of Obligation, Ginny and I went to church that morning of December 8, at the pink Cathedral in Baguio high on the hill opposite Holy Ghost Hill. We had heard bombs and strafing that morning, but, like everyone else, we thought the American soldiers were practicing at Camp John Hay.

In the middle of the Consecration, we heard more loud thumping sounds. The priest put down the chalice and told everyone to go home. He advised that we hide in ditches if we heard the planes again.

We went back to the convent, where everything was quiet. Some Igorots came to the door to sell strawberries and sugarcane. While I was washing the fruit in the kitchen, I heard the same loud pounding that we had heard while at church—the Japanese were attacking Baguio! The bombs terrified me, but Ginny and one of the nuns ran outside, to the point of the hill, and watched the attacking planes.

That evening, two U.S. officers stopped by Holy Ghost Hill to thank the nuns for their prayers. The rear fender of their army car was pockmarked with shrapnel. I don't know exactly why they stopped by, perhaps to thank God that more damage hadn't resulted, or possibly to give directions on what to do now that the Japanese were on their way. The Filipino girls who worked at the convent were crying, fearful that several of the German nuns would be taken away.

We practiced blackouts, covering all windows with dark blankets so that no light showed. We ate spaghetti in a closet by candlelight, and waited …

CHAPTER FOUR

Escape to Manila

Dec. 20 or so, *1941*

ONE EVENING ABOUT A WEEK LATER, on short notice, the mine ordered that all women and children be evacuated by bus to the safety of Manila. Since Ginny and I were not living at the mine, it was not possible for us to make the bus in time. So the next day our dad, who was still at the mine, called us at Holy Ghost to say he had arranged a ride for us in a company car, telling us not to worry about him—he would follow as soon as possible.

Two men from the mine, armed with pistols, drove Ginny and me down the mountain. We took one suitcase each and an egg sandwich for lunch. As we approached the flatlands, the men surveyed the landscape, very alert, looking for enemy soldiers who had reportedly landed on nearby beachheads. I later learned that gold bullion from the mine was in the trunk, to be whisked away on the submarine U.S.S. *Trout* to Australia and then the United States.

In Manila we tried to return to Holy Ghost, but were told that, even though our beds had been made in a room above the laundry and in another building, there was no space for us (the military may have been concerned that the Japanese would attack the building; it's also said that the U.S. Army was using part of it as a hospital), so we were sent to a nearby European orphanage, probably St. Anthony's Convent (which no longer exists), at least until conditions permitted us to return to Holy Ghost. There we stayed in the dormitory with the other kids. I remember a cute little blond German girl, maybe four or five years old. A nun once asked the little girl how much she loved her and she responded, "Up to the heavens." I was taken by the response, thinking how sad it would be to be an orphan.

We were treated well. One evening, as we were preparing for bed, a bat showed up. I was the only one who had put down her mosquito net, so all the girls ran for cover under my net.

On December 22, the main Imperial Army force of 43,000 men landed at Lingayen Gulf, 100 miles north of Manila. On December 23, the first bombs fell inside Manila, aimed at ships in the bay and in the Pasig River, as well as the facilities in the port area.

During this time, our father left Baguio for Manila. Possessing only the clothes on his back and the few belongings that he could carry, he, and the men he was traveling with, could see the Japanese about 20 minutes behind them. He walked, thumbing a ride when he could, at long last reaching Manila. Around Christmas he visited Ginny and me at the orphanage, then he went to stay at the Elks Club. It was months before we saw him again.

We celebrated Christmas at the orphanage. I was given a cute, store-bought stuffed deer made of red cloth with white dots on its back. The only military action was an unexpected air raid late on Christmas night.

With the Japanese making strong headway into their invasion, clear they couldn't be stopped, MacArthur realized he had lost the advantage. He had an army of more than 100,000 men on Luzon, 70,000 of them Filipino Scouts, many of whom he'd brought from other islands to defend the capital. But they were ill-equipped, many using rifles and helmets that dated from World War I. The Filipinos also lacked training and, in some cases, shoes. With orders from President Roosevelt to hold the Philippines for as long as possible without help from the U.S., MacArthur gave up the military's Rainbow-5 plan and activated the original War Plan Orange—essentially, withdrawing his government, the troops, and the Philippine government across Manila Bay to Bataan and the heavily fortified island of Corregidor, and leaving the rest of the Philippines to fend for itself.

Preparing for the Japanese invasion, the Americans set storage facilities and refineries on fire, the oil creating heavy black clouds over Manila that spotted drying laundry and left a black, greasy film on everything—explaining the Filipino reference to Black

Christmas that year. I recall a lot of smoke billowing up on the other side of the orphanage's wall and being told that books at the university were being burned in a large bonfire.

In the hopes of saving it from death and destruction, MacArthur proclaimed Manila an Open City on December 26:

"In order to spare the Metropolitan area from ravages of attack, either by air or ground, Manila is hereby declared an open city without the characteristics of a military objective. In order that no excuse may be given for possible mistake, the American high commissioner, the Commonwealth government and all combatant military installations will be withdrawn from its environs as rapidly as possible. The Municipal government will continue to function with its police powers, reinforced by constabulary troops, so that the normal protection of life and property may be preserved. Citizens are requested to maintain obedience to constituted authorities and continue the normal processes of business."

That night, the blackout ended, and Manila blazed with lights. Two large banners were strung across City Hall: "Open City" and "No Shooting."

But the Japanese bombed Manila anyway. On December 27, they struck ships in Manila Bay and up and down the Pasig River, Fort Santiago, and the piers. In the process, scores of historic buildings were destroyed, including many in Intramuros, the old Spanish walled city. Among the architectural victims was the Church of Santo Domingo, a 1590 landmark filled with ancient relics.

MacArthur contacted Washington: "The enemy's present actions can only be deemed completely violative of all the civilized processes of international law. At the proper time I bespeak due retaliatory measures."

On the air on December 29 he told frightened American listeners in the Philippines:

"Do not follow the army to Bataan or Corregidor. Get together in groups rather than be taken as individual families. Destroy any papers showing a connection with the U.S. Military Reserves. Pour all intoxicating beverages down the sink. May God be with you — I shall return."

The American and Filipino troops left their defensive stance of the beachheads, barely escaping as they withdrew to Bataan. Food that should have been transferred from Manila to Bataan fell into Japanese hands. And soon after, so did innocent Allied citizens left in the wake…

MacArthur wholeheartedly believed that Washington had not forsaken him when, in essence, it had. Roosevelt had every intention of providing the Pacific theater with only 15 percent of available money, men, and materiel until Hitler was crushed.

On January 2, 1942, at 8 p.m., the Imperial forces marched into Manila. The first Japanese rode bikes, with guns strapped to their backs, followed by motor vehicles. Japanese flags went up over the High Commissioner's residence; Fort Santiago; U.S. Army headquarters at the mouth of the river; Malacañang Palace, the official home of the president of the Philippines; the Army and Navy Club; and the adjoining Elks Club. Japanese sentries were stationed in pairs at all main street intersections, and in front of clubs, hotels, and apartment houses.

Americans and other Allies were informed by radio and loudspeaker to stay indoors and pack a blanket, mosquito net, and clothing for three days. More than 3,000 Allied civilians who had the misfortune of being in the Philippines at that time — CEOs, cruise ship passengers, bankers, teachers, diplomats, and, among them, unbeknownst to Ginny and me, our father — were thereby picked up at their homes and in their hotels by the Japanese soldiers and transported to the University of Santo Tomas, which was being used as a retainment area. Soon this ancient, revered campus would become known to the world as Santo Tomas Internment Camp, home to its prisoners for the next three years of war.

CHAPTER FIVE

❖

War

1942-1945

IN EARLY JANUARY 1942, some Japanese men came to visit the orphanage. Even though one of them was a priest, we believed they had come to take us into a concentration camp. We didn't really know what that meant, only that it was happening to Americans and Europeans across Manila. Ginny and I could not stop our tears of fright.

Recently, someone asked me how did I manage my fears? "We clung closely to each other," I told her. "Ever since our mother died."

At the end of January, Ginny and I returned to Holy Ghost College. Wearing beige and white uniforms that were washed and ironed for us, we went to class with fellow Filipino girls. We learned Tagalog, Japanese, and how to weave baskets, as well as academic subjects. We went to Mass.

We stayed in a huge dorm, with two rows of beds. Like the other children, we each had a bed and a small cabinet holding our belongings. A nun slept at the end of one of the rows in a closed cubicle. Beautiful capiz shell squares within wooden panels composed the windows of one entire wall. We used a communal bathroom off the hallway, with one long basin and individual spigots spaced along the way and individual showers.

Canned goods, leftover from the U.S. Army, were stored in some of the classrooms, with signs posted to warn anyone from entering. At one point, the enemy hauled away the food; spying from a window, I was appalled to see a Japanese man open a can and eat its contents without silverware.

One day three or four Japanese women showed up and, whoever they were, lived with us in the dormitory. They were gracious and nice. I was a little wary of them, though Ginny was friendly. One gave Ginny and me cute toy dogs with white fur.

Every school day we went outside to do exercises that were instructed over a loudspeaker, listening to Japanese songs and the new Filipino national anthem. We memorized the educational mandates of the Greater East Asia Co-Prosperity Sphere, the Japanese scheme to keep Asia Asian. One of our homework assignments was to paste (using cooked rice) pieces of paper over anything American or relating to the Commonwealth of the Philippines — words, dollar signs, etc. Complete stories had been cut out of our readers. The books looked rather toothless.

Generally, we were not allowed off the grounds of Holy Ghost College, but there were exceptions. Once we were taken to visit soldiers in a hospital, to provide morale (I assume). Americans were supposed to wear armbands for identification, which Ginny and I didn't have. Walking back to Holy Ghost, we passed a sentry at San Beda next door. "Are they Allemagne or Americano?" the sentry demanded either in Spanish or Tagalog, probably the former. I was terrified. I couldn't speak. The quick-thinking Filipina we were with responded, "Allemagne."

Another time I walked with my class to a radio station and sang songs on the air in Japanese, as well as a German one translated into English about a jolly huntsman. We also ate lunch at the home of a Chinese woman, who lived in our dorm at school.

Meantime, Japan sought to conquer East Asia, destroying or neutralizing American striking power in the Pacific — after Pearl Harbor and the Philippines, they moved south and east to take over Malaya, the Netherlands Indies, Wake Island, Guam, the Gilbert Islands, Thailand, and Burma. At first, their strategy worked.

The Americans fought bravely on Corregidor and Bataan for five months, with MacArthur giving orders from Malinta Tunnel on Corregidor. When it became clear that Bataan was going to fall, Roosevelt ordered MacArthur to escape by gunboat to Australia. The general left on March 12, 1942, uttering his famous words upon arriving in Australia: "I shall return!" Forsaken by the U.S., the "Battling Bastards of Bataan" said they had "no Mama, no Papa, and no Uncle Sam." Two months after Bataan fell, on May 6, Corregidor was surrendered. The abandoned Filipino and American soldiers, already dehydrated, malnourished, sick with dysentery and malaria, were forced to march beneath the beating sun, without food or water, for five days in the infamous Bataan Death March. The ill and weak fell by the wayside, dying on the spot or killed by Japanese bayonets and clubs.

Ginny and I were safe behind the walls of Holy Ghost College, but even there, wartime secrets waited to be discovered. Once, probably about April 1942, I was swinging in the playground. I heard music, so I swung high enough to look over the wall. There I saw Japanese trucks and American soldiers on Mendiola Street—it was a Japanese victory parade to celebrate Bataan's surrender. Another parade took place later, too, after Corregidor surrendered.

Sometimes, when I practiced piano on the second floor of Holy Ghost's Music Building, I slid down the bench to peek under the curtain. Once I saw a work detail at neighboring San Beda; a captured American soldier was being clubbed. Another time I saw American women standing on chairs, peering through the tennis courts' foliage, watching for a possible glimpse of a husband or loved one who might be part of that work detail.

Hearing these stories, someone recently asked me how did I handle it all as a nine-year-old girl. "To close up, to be invisible," I told her.

Dr. Fay del Mundo, who had done postgraduate work at Harvard Medical School and, after the war, went on to found the first pediatric hospital in the Philippines, worked out a deal so that some 400 kids imprisoned at the University of Santo Tomas could come and live at Holy Ghost, in the Holy Ghost Home for Children (in a different building from the one that Ginny and I were living in). The nuns felt that some of the kids were loud and used language they didn't want us to hear, so they limited the time we were allowed to play with them. In the afternoon at 4:00, Ginny and

I would go to their building for milk and vitamins.

The good news is that the kids' parents were bused in to visit from time to time, and Dad could get a ride. It was a happy time, when we saw our father again. We made swords out of bamboo and played by the grotto, almost as if a war wasn't swirling all around us. Once we visited Santo Tomas Internment Camp and had an ice-cream cone. The camp was a busy place.

Why did the Japanese allow the American kids to live outside the camp? Because they were winning, and the parents thought it good to get them out of the camp environment. As time progressed, though, as it became evident that the Americans were effectively pushing back the Japanese, and the Japanese feared they may lose the war, the visits became fewer and fewer, until there were none.

The Japanese had expected the United States to negotiate peace, not strike back. But the United States did just that. First MacArthur turned back the Japanese attempt to use New Guinea as a springboard for an invasion of Australia. Successful there, he began his island-hopping campaign in which he attacked and conquered vulnerable islands, leaving large enemy forces cut off on more fortified islands while moving the front north, ever closer to Japan.

In January 1944, as the tide of war in the Pacific Theater began to change in favor of the Americans, the Japanese Military Police took control of the camp—and life became more miserable for the prisoners. On March 10, 1944, the enemy decided that Ginny and I should be brought into Santo Tomas. Also at that time, others who had been allowed to stay outside were brought inside, including nuns, the infirmed, and mestizos.

As soon as it became evident that we would be imprisoned, Ginny and I were hastily confirmed at the Cathedral in Manila, both taking the name Mary.

CHAPTER SIX
❖

Santo Tomas Internment Camp
1944-1945

BEFORE THE WAR, the University of Santo Tomas was best known for being Asia's oldest university. Indeed, founded in 1611 by the Dominican Fathers and invested with the power to confer degrees by Pope Paul V, it's older than Harvard. The university moved to a new 65-acre campus in North Manila in 1927, an imposing cluster of buildings surrounded on all sides by a high wall or iron fence. The principal buildings included the Main Building, with its tower rising in a boxlike mass topped by a cross, and the Education Building, both of which consisted mainly of classrooms; plus a gymnasium and two light construction, one-story buildings called the Annex and Infirmary.

We left Holy Ghost for Santo Tomas via calesa (horse-drawn carriage), with our luggage following by truck—one suitcase each, and a mattress. The Japanese inspected our luggage in front of the Main Building, and it passed without incident. Dad met us and helped carry our belongings to the third floor of the Main Building.

By this time, the camp held 3,800 Allied civilians as prisoners of war, mostly housed in the classrooms that had been converted into overcrowded dormitories. We were shown to Room 55A on the third floor, a corner room home to 26 women and children—guests of the Japanese Imperial Army. We were directed to our allocated spaces midway in the room, to the right of the door. Each space measured three feet by eight feet, enough room for a bed (averaging three feet by six feet) and not much more. A friend of our dad's later made little wooden blocks to lift our beds higher, so we could have room for our suitcases and a place to hide during air raids.

Among the prisoners in Room 55A were two girls around my age, Connie Ford and Dorothy (Dot) Mullaney, the latter just a month older than me and even in the same grade. Upon our arrival,

Dot promptly showed me around, telling me where everything was located. The bathrooms were down the hall, where curtains hung instead of doors, and there was little privacy.

An Executive Committee of nine internees, approved by the Japanese Commandant, had been established in 1942 at the beginning of internment to oversee the running of the camp. Some of these men had met together before the occupation at the prospect of being imprisoned, just in case, to start making plans. Chaired by Earl Carroll, president of the Philippine-American Life Insurance Company, they established different committees to oversee every aspect of the internees' lives—laundry, dishwashing, food, etc. The whole place was run like a small city.

Everyone had a responsibility. Our father taught first aid and worked on the garbage detail. Dot's father, who volunteered at the canteen, would on occasion give us a handful of peanuts when he was working there. One time he gave us a duck egg that we almost overcooked in the hot pan!

Our days were organized into various activities, beginning with roll call. In Room 55A, Connie Ford's mother lined us up every morning, where we would occasionally have to stand for hours. I got the food and hand washed both Ginny's and my sheets and clothes with cold water at an outdoor laundry tub. Once a month we could use the iron in a room down the hall.

Among the most important events of the day, of course, was chow time, when, about an hour before food was ladled out, I'd stand with our dad's and my meal tickets and our tin cans with wire handles, waiting for the line to open. I'd then have our tickets punched and be served. (Ginny ate at the children's line.)

Initially, when the camp opened in 1941, the Japanese had made no provisions for feeding their prisoners. At that time, those with money could buy food from Filipinos through the iron bars along Calle España, and a package line was established to allow people in the Manila community to pass food and sundries, clothes, laundry, beds, mattresses, even home-cooked meals, to their imprisoned friends. The Executive Committee eventually established a committee to purchase food in the camp from the outside community, and a central kitchen was set up to feed everyone. The Philippine Red Cross provided funds at first, but the Japanese eventually found ways to divert these funds and supplies. The Japanese then agreed to pay a stipend that was considerably less than what had previously been provided by the Red Cross. Quality and quantity of food declined with the lower food allowance and as shortages and inflation reduced the amount of food that could be obtained. This plan continued until early 1944, when the Japanese Military Police took control of the camp (and when Ginny and I were forced to enter), and the food purchasing committee was forbidden to leave the camp. At that time, the Japanese started allocating food to the prisoners.

Breakfast and dinner were often a watery stew of talinum (green leafy weed), camotes (sweet potatoes), corn, some soy, and watery rice—called lugao (coconut milk was sometimes added for breakfast). Meat was scarce—though once I found a small piece of carabao hide in my lugao. Sometimes we were given a small canful of dry fish at lunch, ground-up and mixed with water. It was dark brown and very salty. Even though I was hungry, I couldn't stomach the soupy fish. I gave it to my father and sister and instead ate porridge that I had saved from breakfast, to which I added more water to fill me up.

For a little while there was a special line for teenagers (teenage years beginning at 11), so on June 18, 1944, my 11th birthday, I went into that line.

Even in prison, we attended school, from 8 a.m. to noon, five days a week. One advantage of imprisoning Manila's expats was the high caliber of professional teachers available to teach classes from kindergarten to twelfth grade; Don Holter headed the impromptu school. Since Holy Ghost followed a different school year, and I didn't want to repeat the part I'd already finished, I was given several pages of information to study and be tested on for placement purposes. It was mostly history questions: Who was Columbus? What were the names of his three ships? I was placed in sixth grade. Classes were held in rooms on the fourth floor, the top floor that had been the university's labs. I studied ancient history and I wrote stories inspired by pictures torn out of a magazine.

In our free time, Ginny and I and our friends climbed on a bamboo jungle gym at the playground and played on something called a "giant stride"—a giant pole with several ropes hanging down from the top. We would grab a rope and run in a circle, going faster and faster until our feet were flying in the air. On Mondays we took acrobatic dancing classes. We played Monopoly with friends (often resulting in a squabble—like there wasn't enough fighting with war all around us). Connie climbed the little trees in front of the Main Building, until they disappeared for firewood over time. As food became more scarce, the playground was converted into a vegetable garden. We were liberated before my okra was ready to be eaten. (However, that little patch did serve as a foxhole for one of the American soldiers during the Battle of Manila.) Toward the end, many people shared recipes. I wrote them down on yellow Japanese cigarette wrappers that had blown off a truck that came into camp.

One day I found a tired rubber dolly in the trash. I took it, washed it, and hand sewed clothes for it—a gathered skirt or jumper with straps.

Supplies of clothing came from Red Cross shipments; local Red Cross boxes packed just before the war to help those who needed them also found their way into camp. Mainly, though, people wore whatever they could find; they mended their few items as best they could. Ginny and I both had dresses with the letters U.S.A. embroidered on the front; but we hid those away for fear of angering the Japanese guards. When my feet grew, I had to cut off the toes of my shoes, because there were no other shoes. We also wore *bakyas*—a wooden sole with a strip of car tire nailed to the front.

On Sundays we attended Mass, first in the small Santa Catalina hospital chapel, then in the balconied museum room of the Main Building. I passed time staring at the stuffed animals, including a hairy orangutan and a two-headed baby carabao.

Until July 1, 1944, Dave Harvey, a Shanghai entertainer and

NORTHERN CALIFORNIA *Top: Leanne and her dad at their home near the Dewey Gold Mine, northern California. Bottom left: Leanne at 7 months and 1 week on the front porch of the Blinzler home near the Dewey Gold Mine. Bottom right: Ginny and Leanne at San Francisco's Marina.*

NORTHERN CALIFORNIA *Leanne and Ginny with Kay, at the Booth's house in San Francisco, in 1935 or 1936.*

PRE-WAR *Clockwise from right: Leanne, Ginny, and Lee at Holy Ghost Hill, Baguio; Leanne on a horse at Burnham Park, Baguio; Leanne, Ginny, and the other students in Baguio, May 1940; Leanne's First Communion, September 8, 1940.*

MANILA *Opposite: Lee, Leanne, and Ginny at the grotto pond, Holy Ghost College, Manila, 1937.*

SANTO TOMAS INTERNMENT CAMP *This page, left: Lee kept these two photos of Kay and the girls close to him throughout the entire time in the prison camp. Below: Some of the STIC shanties.*

STIC

Top: The list of prisoner laws on the front gate of Santo Tomas, 1944 or 1945. Middle: A Japanese propaganda image of Margaret Whitaker (right) doing laundry in Los Baños. Right: Picture of rescued internees Lee Rogers and John C. Todd that appeared in Time. *Opposite: Former prisoners in front of Santo Tomas during MacArthur's visit.*

BATTLE OF MANILA Top: *Santo Tomas being shelled by the Japanese in the days after Liberation.* Bottom: *Manila was the second most devastated city in World War II, after Warsaw, Poland.*

LIBERATION AND HEADING HOME

Left: Leanne and a marine on the Admiral Capps. *Below:* New York Times *story about life on the* Admiral Capps; *Ginny (wearing the sailor cap) and Leanne are on the right.*

HEADING HOME
Right: Ginny made the news! Some of the information in the story is incorrect, including the fact that the girls were hit at Holy Ghost Convent and that they were en route to live with their grandmother. Below: Family Reunited: Lee's brothers, sisters, their spouses, and Granny's sister, Rose Lauer, at Granny Blinzler's house in Buffalo, 1945.

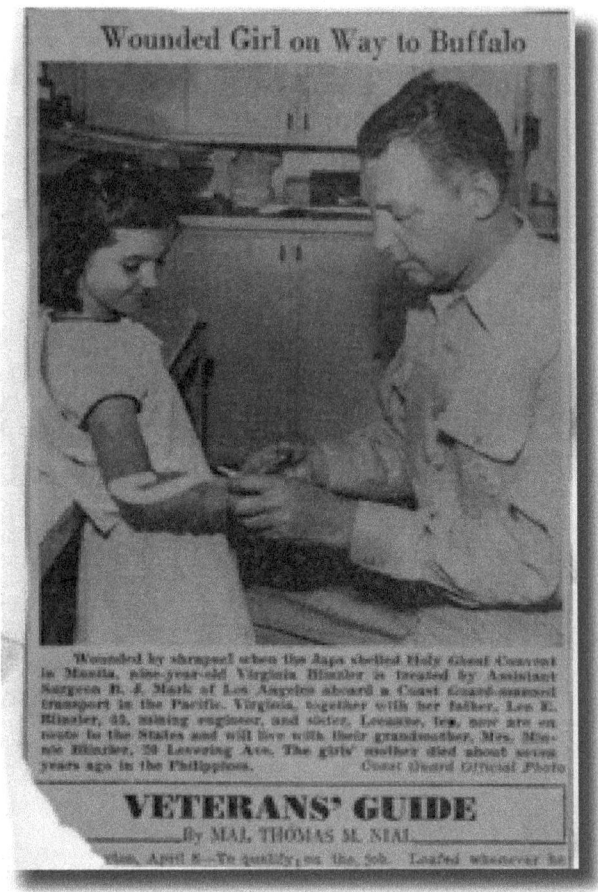

AFTER THE WAR
Top: Leanne and daughter Barbara (third and fourth from left) at Holy Ghost, 2005. Center: En route to the mine outside Baguio, 2005. Left: Image of the mine that appeared on Lee's Christmas card one year.

2005 VISIT *Top: Roommates together again – Connie, Dot, and Leanne in front of their classroom/prison in 2005. Above right: Modern-day photo of the Santo Tomas classroom where Leanne slept with 25 others during the war. Above left: Two-headed caribou that is still on display.*

professional comedian, established "theater under the stars." A huge screen and wooden stage were set up on the grounds, and we watched Abbott and Costello, the Three Stooges, and Japanese propaganda films. Each audience member brought their own seat and enjoyed an evening of entertainment; though the reels sometimes broke. There was also a mixture of acts, quiz contests, singing, dancing, instrumental concerts, and Harvey's comedy routines. There were songs about meals, crowding, and rumors of release, and bedbugs. (Bedbugs were a huge problem in camp. Everyone scratched their bites and killed other bugs that clung to the mosquito nets. We would eat on a bench outside Dad's room and received a few bites there as well.)

Even though we were prisoners, I have fond memories—of my friends, the games we played, and the fact that Ginny and I could eat meals with our father every day.

Some families were allowed to live or spend the day in small shanties around the campus. Dot's family had a shanty in the East Patio of the Main Building. These little huts, about ten feet square, made out of tin, wood, bamboo, and sawali matting, needed to be open on at least two sides. Some were built on stilts, beneath which the occupants dug out an air-raid shelter (everyone else took shelter in the hallways of the Annex or Main Building during air raids). Others just had a dirt floor, which became muddy during rain. Inside, shanty residents sometimes cooked over a charcoal stove and sat around rough tables on folding stools.

There were rules, including no lovemaking. (Forty-two babies, however, were born during three years of war; fathers of the new babies were placed in prison in the front hall of the Main Building.)

Over time, the shanties were divided into villages—including Glamorville (considered the best), Barrio Foggy Bottom, Jungletown, and Shanty Town—each with its own elected mayor. Streets were created as well, including Picadilly Circus, Fifth Avenue, and Lexington Avenue. Until the camp became overcrowded, they could only be inhabited during the day; residents would then have to sleep in the university buildings.

❖ ❖ ❖

After more than two years of tough fighting across the southwest Pacific, MacArthur was faced with a choice: invade the Philippines, or hopscotch farther north to Formosa (Taiwan). Other military officials had argued that Formosa was a more strategic plan, since it was located 600 miles south of Japan itself. But MacArthur clung to his belief that capturing the Philippines would make a Formosa invasion easier; he declared that he could take Luzon in December 1944, while a Formosa invasion would not be ready to launch until February 1945. In addition, with the help of the Filipinos and guerillas, a large number of occupation forces would not be expended in a Filipino invasion. Bottom line: Taking the Philippines would be cheaper than Formosa.

On October 3, 1944, MacArthur's new plan was accepted. He chose to invade the island of Leyte rather than the principal island of Luzon as the initial landing site.

On the 20th of that month, MacArthur's troops stormed ashore along Leyte's east coast. The general put on a fresh uniform and boarded a landing craft for the beach, only to go aground in shallow water about 35 yards from shore. With snipers taking pot shots from the palm groves and light fighting going on about half a mile inland, there was no time to switch to a smaller craft. So MacArthur and his party waded ashore in one of the most famous photo opportunities of the war. MacArthur later wrote, "That was one of the most meaningful walks I ever took."

On the beach, he gave a two-minute speech:

"People of the Philippines, I have returned. By the grace of Almighty God our forces stand again on Philippine soil ... the hour of your redemption is here. Your patriots have demonstrated an unswerving and resolute devotion to the principles of freedom ... Rally to me. Let the indomitable spirit of Bataan and Corregidor lead on. As the lines of battle roll forward to bring you within the zone of operations, rise and strike ... For future generations of your sons and daughters, strike! In the name of your sacred dead, strike! Let no heart be faint. Let every arm be steeled."

His words and photos traveled around the world, giving hope that the U.S. military might possibly be recovering from its early disasters.

As time wore on, the food in the camp got worse. Eventually, meals were limited to two a day and to two lines—the annex (children's) and the grown-up line; the teenage line was closed. I thought the food in the grown-up line was not as good as that in the annex, where my sister still ate. As food supplies became more scarce, beri beri, dengue fever, dysenteries, and other diseases caused by nutritional deficiencies were resulting in more and more deaths. I tried to eat a hibiscus flower once but found it too slimy. Our dad forbade us from scooping up any drops of food from the concrete floor of the "chow line."

The internees survived through rumors, and hope. Every morning we were awakened by a song on the PA system, and if we listened carefully, we might glean some information about the war's progress, culled by prisoners who had set up an illicit correspondence network. There was a rumor, for example, that Hitler died. The next morning, it was essentially confirmed with the song "Ding Dong the Witch is Dead."

We knew the Americans were getting close in September 1944, with the first air raid on the 21st. It was so exciting to be rushed out of class. The next morning, the song on the PA system was "Every Time I Pray It Rains," another sign of hope.

The day after MacArthur and his men landed on Leyte in October 1944, rumors ran crazily around the campus. Everyone waited in anticipation to see what would be played over the PA system. Seven a.m. came, 7:10, 7:15 … What was going on? People began to think that something bad had happened. Then music began, and the announcer said: "Oops, better Leyte than never!" The rumors were confirmed.

Early on, when the first air raids occurred—a sign that the Americans were getting closer—we rushed from the fourth-floor classrooms down the stairs to our rooms as quietly but as hastily as we could. One time my books were scattered, so I learned to keep them in order so they could be picked up at a moment's notice. In our rooms, we crawled under our beds, placing a wooden block in our mouths to protect ourselves from a concussion, and cotton in our ears. Before too long, however, we felt safe from falling shrapnel and bombs and I joined the others in watching the planes until a sentry yelled at me. People were punished for doing that.

After air raids, Ginny and I ran outside to collect shrapnel. One day I found a decent size piece. I put it in a pouch with pockets tied at the foot of the bed, where I kept my toothpaste and toothbrush. Then, over the loudspeaker came the announcement: Some of the shrapnel was still alive! I was too scared to go fetch it and asked someone else to throw it out.

Another time, when we were in class and before the air-raid siren sounded to go downstairs, I saw a dogfight. An American plane went down; the next day, planes came by in formation, creating a smoke wreath in commemoration. As air raids became more common, the Japanese guards punished any prisoner caught watching them by making them stand in front of the Main Building in the hot sun for hours.

As the war wore on, the Japanese reduced food supplies to 800 calories per day, and by the end of 1944, death by starvation and related diseases increased rapidly. I experienced horrible hunger pains, crying myself to sleep at night. Ten or so people a day died from malnutrition. Dr. Stevenson, the camp doctor, signed the cause of demise on each death certificate with the true cause, which the Japanese did not like. He was thrown into prison—a room to the left of the main entrance in the Main Building. I joined others outside the room to let him know we were there for him. By the time of our liberation, 400 people had died from malnutrition.

On the subject of tragic demises, during our imprisonment seven people were executed, one died in a fight, and 18 died from enemy action. At the beginning of internment three men who had gone over the wall were caught; they were forced to dig their own grave, and then they were shot, their bodies toppling into the freshly dug hole. As the crowd dispersed, a sole Japanese guard stood there and threw bougainvillea flowers into the grave.

And toward the end of internment, four of the camp leaders

were picked up. At first they were placed in the camp's front hall prison and then later taken out of camp. We did not know why and could not get any answers from the Japanese. After Liberation it was discovered that they had been beheaded and buried. We remember C. C. Grinnell, A. F. Duggleby, C. L. Larsen, and E. E. Johnson.

The good news is that the American bombing and air raids continued more frequently. By mid-December 1944 U.S. Armed Forces had landed on Mindoro, just south of Luzon, putting the United States in position for an early January 1945 landing at Lingayen Gulf.

On Christmas, I received a piece of *bucayo*, coconut brown sugar candy. Our dad talked about how much better next Christmas would be. He always kept our hopes alive.

That same Christmas, a leaflet was dropped into camp, reading: "The Commander in Chief, the Officers and the Men of the American Forces of Liberation in the Pacific wish their gallant allies, the People of the Philippines, all the blessings of Christmas and the realization of their fervent hopes for the New Year."

On January 10, 1945, another leaflet was dropped: "The Battle of the Philippines is in its final phase ..."

CHAPTER SEVEN

Liberation
Feb. 3, 1945

IN SUMMER 1944, THE AMERICANS intercepted a secret advisory from Tokyo to local commanders in the Philippines, declaring that in the case of an imminent rescue of any Allied internees, the prisoners should be killed immediately—by decapitation, drowning, or however else the job could be done.

Was there a plan to kill the internees of Santo Tomas on February 6? No one can confirm this rumor for sure, though it's said that American intelligence received a message from a clandestine radio in Santo Tomas stating that the Japanese appeared to be preparing to execute the prisoners. Whatever the case, MacArthur knew the Japanese mind; he had followed battles throughout Southeast Asia and China, where, time and again, as U.S. forces advanced, prisoners in the immediate area were killed. One of the most chilling examples occurred on Dec. 14, 1944, on the island of Palawan. One hundred and fifty prisoners were detained in their wooden air-raid shelters, which were doused with airplane fuel and lit on fire. As the men rushed out of the buildings, the Japanese waited for them with bayonets, machine guns, and clubs. Only 11 men survived.

As such, upon landing at Lingayen Gulf in early January, MacArthur was adamant that the First Cavalry move on to Manila as quickly as possible. After the military POW camp of Cabanatuan was freed on January 30 in a thrilling raid by U.S. Army Rangers, Alamo Scouts, and Filipino guerillas, he ordered fully seasoned combat troops to speed down to the Japanese-occupied capital and Santo Tomas, the largest internment camp in the Philippines, rather than continue the reconquest of Luzon.

From Guimba, a "flying column" comprising about 700 men, a tank company, a battery of 105-mm howitzers, and armored vehicles to carry all, charged south down Highway 5, across the

Luzon plain, sometimes reaching up to 30 miles an hour on the highways, sometimes forced to a crawl along carabao trails. If they came across a bridge that had been blown up, they forded the river, weapons overhead. At one point, a makeshift bridge was built in record time. They halted only to fight off ambushing Japanese. In a mere 66 hours, the flying column traveled 100 miles to reach Manila. Within 72 hours, they had reached the closed walls of Santo Tomas, an imposing concrete barrier a quarter mile long and 10 feet high.

Lt. Diosdado Guytingco
Words of a true hero

When my eldest daughter, Barbara, and I visited the Philippines in 2005 as part of a prisoner-of-war reunion to celebrate the sixtieth anniversary of our liberation, we met one of the guerillas who led the American tanks that night to Santo Tomas. Lt. Diosdado Guytingco was 23 years old, part of the guerilla force that was gathering information on troop movements in and out of Manila.

"On February 3," he told us at a special lunch at Santo Tomas, "I met the First Cavalry and guided them down Rizal Avenue." As they approached the walled campus of Santo Tomas, he said, Lt. Col. Haskett "Hack" Conner, who headed the column, asked him to run to the front near the wall and look for the commanding officer, Capt. Manuel Colayco. Guytingco did as he was told, and there he saw two jeeps followed by the tanks. They were surveying Santo Tomas's layout and the location of the Japanese guards. "I was scared," he told us. "I am not a brave man."

All of a sudden, a Japanese grenade came over the wall, falling in the middle of the column. Lieutenant Colonel Conner was hit in the knee by shrapnel, but "my captain [Colayco] was badly injured; he had shrapnel holes in his body," Guytingco said. "When the smoke of the explosion was over, Captain Colayco was not able to stand." Guytingco carried him to the grass, then ran down the column, looking for the medic. "Colayco was saying, 'I feel cold, I feel cold.' I gave him my shirt."

Captain Colayco would die seven days later. Lieutenant Colonel Conner, despite his wounds, ordered the lead tank to attack the gate. "That's when the fighting started," Guytingco said.

The tanks of the 44th Battalion in the First Cavalry, first the *Battlin' Basic*, followed closely by the *Georgia Peach*, crashed into the gates of Santo Tomas. At first the tanks' powerful lights illuminated no sign of life in the darkened structures. Then suddenly the Main Building exploded with lights and the night air filled with joyful shouts. The tanks moved up the long driveway, accompanied by foot soldiers and the guerillas who had led the First Cavalry to the building. There was bedlam.

Battlin' Basic
Words of another hero

John Hencke, the corporal in the head tank that broke down the gate of Santo Tomas—the *Battlin' Basic*—spoke at a POW reunion that Barbara and I attended in San Antonio in 2001, recalling the events of that night. "I saw a sparkle come over the fence and yelled 'Grenade!'" he said. "As the tank crept through the wall, I didn't close the hatch because it was so dark. 'Does anyone have any light?' I yelled. I looked down and saw a man in a white robe with long hair and long beard, carrying a shepherd staff. I wouldn't swear he was barefoot, but..." Someone suggested it may have been one of the Dominican fathers who somehow had gotten there from a neighboring building. No matter what or who the apparition was, miracles occurred that night.

Earlier that day of February 3, anticipation raced throughout the camp. Planes were flying low—not the typical bombers but tiny Piper cubs with blue stars on silver backgrounds ... Americans!

We were told to stay inside our building. There wasn't a lot of activity—just whispered speculation. Smoke wafted from buildings around the camp—the adults were overheard saying that the Japanese were burning their records.

After dinner, while dishes were being washed, planes flew overhead, and a pilot dropped a pair of goggles with a note: "Roll out the barrel"—referring to a song whose last line is "the gang's all here." The planes left, and everyone returned to their chores. There was a 6 o'clock roll call and early bedtime. Continuous machine-gun fire could be heard to the north. I could see the light from tracer bullets streaking across the sky through the windows. I heard low rumblings, gunfire in the distance, and the black sky lit up like the northern lights.

Then, someone said that an American tank was striking through the wall outside the camp. People started poking their heads out of the windows, wondering, what was that? The Japanese warned over the loud speaker to stay away from the windows, and the shanty dwellers were ordered to seek cover in the Main Building. The whole camp went dark.

At 9:00, without warning, the plaza in front of the Main Building lit up with pink and white flares. Ginny and I rushed down to the front hall—Ginny lost one of her slippers in her rush. Normally, this would have been upsetting, but not tonight! We watched from the crowded stairs in the lobby of the Main Building's front hall.

Soon, a tank came into view. Everyone was running around and shouting, "They're here! They're here!" The vehicle came to a halt, and several unusually tall and healthy looking men emerged, looking like big, good-natured giants. They were taking atabrine, an antimalarial drug, so their skin had a yellowish tinge.

More tanks arrived, with more American soldiers. They greeted the prisoners like old friends and offered the kids candy, cigarettes for the adults. Gen. William C. Chase stood up on a table in the lobby: "I'm so glad to see you," he said. "Better to give life than take life."

The former prisoners were warned to stay inside the building. The Japanese officer Abiko, in charge of the prisoners and food, the most hated Japanese soldier, was poised outside the Main Building to throw a hand grenade. An American soldier saw and shot him before anyone was hurt.

Ginny and I ran upstairs to our dad's room on the third floor. Kerosene lamps lit the halls—the first time in months that the complete blackout wasn't being observed. He wasn't there; trained in first aid, he was downstairs where his help might be needed. So we returned to our room on the second floor.

Ruth Harrington, whose bed was next to mine, was sitting in the hallway. She had her last 7-ounce tin of ham and eggs, saved from our single American Red Cross comfort kit (though we had been promised one every month, we had only received the one), which she shared with me. A whole half can! Ruth's three-year-old daughter Patricia was already asleep in the room. Sadly, her dad, who was in one of the military prison camps, did not survive the war. The Japanese ship he was on was torpedoed by one of our subs.

Back in our room, we were advised to pack a few of our belongings, just in case we had to evacuate at a moment's notice. Outside camp we could see many buildings on fire. Somehow, despite all of the excitement, I soon fell asleep.

Next morning, we were awakened by the loudspeaker, but American songs were playing. And it was one hour later than the usual 6 a.m. rising time.

The breakfast line was quicker, with pails filled three times more than the morning before. I was so eager to get the food to the third floor, where I ate with my sister and dad, that I tripped on the stairs.

After, we went to the plaza to see more of the liberators, who offered us K rations. Ginny was given some bacon, which she tried to eat raw. Someone told her that it needed to be cooked.

Education Building Hostages

An ensuing struggle after liberation of the camp

Meantime, that first night, some Japanese soldiers had managed to find cover on the third floor of the Education Building, where a group of male internees were housed (including Curtis Brooks, who later in life would marry Dot). There were 240 hostages there, on the third floor, all hunkered down. One guy died from a heart attack. According to Curtis, "During the standoff at the Ed Building, the Japanese mingled some with the internees on the third floor, but the situation for them and for us was both tense and for us exhilarating. As far as I know, there was no physical mistreatment of any internees. But no question, we were hostages. We could not leave the building, and shooting at the Japanese meant shooting at us as well. The internees were concentrated on the third floor, at first in the back and then in the front rooms. The Americans fired on the building with machine guns from two or three tanks in front of the building, and also from a machine gun set up on the fourth floor of the Main Building where classes had been held. The Japanese shot back, including, I believe, from positions on the third floor, and at least one crew member on Battlin' Basic was wounded. During the firing, one Japanese was killed, one wounded, and one internee wounded. There was no more firing after about midnight on the 3rd."

Negotiations began. Food was allowed in for everyone. In the end, on February 5, an agreement was reached and the Japanese soldiers were allowed to march out with their weapons, beyond the American line, to a place of their choosing—a place which, unknowingly, happened to be a guerilla stronghold.

Although liberated, the former Santo Tomas prisoners weren't totally in the clear. Caught in the middle of the Battle of Manila, Santo Tomas became a military staging area for tanks and troops, causing the Japanese to continuously shell the camp for nearly two weeks as they tried to regain their foothold. Outside the gates of Santo Tomas, atrocities were committed throughout the city by the Japanese, who raped Filipinas and foreign nuns, stabbed pregnant women, and bayoneted babies. Men were shot on the spot. The American soldiers fought back fiercely with bombs, aircraft, flamethrowers, and grenades. More than a hundred bombs a day were dropped on Intramuros alone, where the Japanese desperately burrowed in defense in historic churches, monasteries, and palaces. Thousands of more Japanese hid east and south of Manila in caves and tunnels. But wherever there were Japanese, near Antipolo, in the Bicol, or in south Luzon, the Americans moved on grimly, forcing the Japanese to retreat beyond the Pasig River. Gradually the Japanese shelling became less frequent as the Americans spotted their artillery and destroyed it.

MacArthur himself paid a brief surprise visit to Santo Tomas on

February 7. In the crowded lobby of the Main Building, he spoke to the crowd of former prisoners: "I'm a little late, but we finally came," he said. During the ceremony, the former prisoners raised the American flag above the entrance of the Main Building—a flag that Dot's father had saved in a pillowcase throughout the entire internment. Everyone joined in singing "God Bless America," a patriotic song forbidden during the Occupation.

As soon as MacArthur left, all heck broke loose. Maybe the Japanese thought he was still there. Many internees and soldiers were wounded, or killed, in the shelling. In the late afternoon of that first day, Curtis Brooks's mother, in Room 3 on the first floor, was in bed, right by the window, when an artillery shell exploded and killed her (Curtis's father had died that same week, from malnutrition). You can still see where Japanese artillery shells hit the south side of the Main Building. Finally, after three days, the Japanese artillery was spotted on the roof of the Philippine General Hospital and efficiently taken out.

The same day MacArthur visited, Ginny and I snuck out past the Military Police. There was a false sense of security, with these big healthy guys standing guard. It was after lunch, nap time, but we were meeting two soldier friends who had promised to give us Hershey bars. All of a sudden, shells rained on the building. Ginny and I were hit, and James Smith carried us both inside. We later learned that the other soldier, Steve Bodo, had been killed.

We were given first aid, loaded on a single stretcher, and taken to the children's library at the back of the Main Building. I looked up as we ascended the stairs to see our dad. He had come down to the first floor to get water when he saw us. He sat silently by our sides the whole afternoon, not saying a word, just being with us. All that night Japanese shelled the camp. It sounded like silk being ripped apart.

We were then transported by Army ambulance to the Quezon Institute in Quezon City, a government building that was now being used as the 54th Evacuation Hospital. I didn't know it then, but I had a piece of shrapnel lodged in my jaw. Ginny's lower arm, just below the elbow, was so damaged by shrapnel that it later required 90 stitches. Her wound was packed with Vaseline gauze and the pain was so excruciating that she had to be put out to change it.

The battle still waged all around us. One day a sniper took a pot shot at us—and missed. And one night the enemy shelled the Evacuation Hospital. During the attack, some of us who were awake sought shelter in the hallway and prayed the rosary, our voices rising up when the shells were closer and louder. An Army nurse named Nancy joined us. I was surprised to see someone in the Army so frightened. The next morning we saw that one of the shells had lodged in the building without exploding.

A butterfly bandage held my wound together. My mouth was so swollen, I could hardly eat. Ginny, with her arm in a sling, gamely kept up with me and other patients there. We would help carry her food tray. The Evacuation Hospital is also where we learned about penicillin—Ginny was given one shot every four hours.

One of the beautiful young women in camp, Veda Tremblay, had been hit in the face and her head was all bandaged with just an opening for her one good eye to see. I also remember seeing an ambulance being loaded with patients who were suffering mental traumas and were being shipped out first for treatment. At Christmas (2010) I still hear from Glen Snider, a soldier we met there.

When we returned to the camp, James Smith, the soldier who had been with us when the shells hit, took us to the temporary grave site of Steve Bodo. (On our return to the States our dad went to visit Steve's parents in New Jersey.) The area to the right of the plaza, in front of the Main Building, had become a temporary cemetery during the Battle of Manila.

Soldiers who had survived New Guinea, the Marianas, and Leyte said Manila was the bloodiest battle they had ever fought. The

Japanese methodically burned and destroyed every building they could. U.S. troops fought street to street in the surrounding areas and, finally, house to house.

By the end, Manila—the beautiful Pearl of the Orient—had been almost completely destroyed by tank, artillery, bombs, and mortar fire. The only building left standing in Intramuros was San Agustin. When all was said and done, Warsaw, Poland, was the only city that experienced greater destruction during World War II.

The symbolic objective was to Retake the Rock—Corregidor, from which MacArthur had fled in 1942. The Americans figured they needed an element of surprise. A parachute drop seemed suicidal, but that's what they decided to do. Two thousand paratroopers took to the skies. The planes had to fly 400 feet above the ground if the men had any hope of hitting the target—a drop zone on the top part of the island that was 200 yards long and several dozen yards wide.

It was estimated that the American casualties would be more than 50 percent; but with little Japanese resistance, only 19 paratroopers died—13 percent.

The final coup de grace: The American soldiers blew up Malinta Tunnel, where the last Japanese had holed up. Before the end of February 1945, MacArthur returned to the Rock.

By July 14, Santo Tomas Internment Camp ended; any remaining internees were transferred to San Carlos Camp. But by then, most former prisoners had already boarded troop ships that took them to the West Coast of the United States and the start of a brand-new life of freedom.

The Amazing Rescue of Los Baños Internment Camp
An account of another well-orchestrated rescue

When Santo Tomas overflowed with too many prisoners, a new prison camp was established in 1943 at the Philippine Agricultural College and Forestry Campus at Los Baños, about 25 miles southeast of Manila. Perched between the foothills of Mount Makliling and the northern shore of Los Baños facing Laguna de Bay, the 60-acre site included a campus gymnasium, where most of the 2,122 internees were incarcerated, as well as rudimentary huts built for the purpose. While the liberation of Santo Tomas is considered one of the most successful rescue missions in war history, the rescue of Los Baños is considered nothing but miraculous.

Guerillas in the area played an important role in providing intelligence about the Los Baños internees and their guards. One important bit of information: The Japanese were planning to execute the POWs on the morning of February 23. Another bit: The off-duty guards exercised at 0700, wearing only loincloths, without equipment or weapons.

On that morning, just as the prisoners were lining up for roll call, a four-phase, multipronged raid went into effect. The prisoners looked up to the skies to see 130 paratroopers from the 11th Airborne Division, submachine guns in hand, dropping into camp. At the same time, strategically placed ground troops attacked the guard posts and guardroom. A quick battle ensued, but the Japanese were quickly defeated and the internees freed. However, they were not safe. They needed to get across the Laguna de Bay, behind U.S. lines, before the infamous Tiger Division, just over the hill, found out what was going on.

There was some confusion. Many prisoners were reluctant to leave camp, so the soldiers lit their huts on fire to persuade them to move quickly. The former prisoners were ushered to waiting amphibious trucks—fifty-four Amtracs of the 672nd Amphibious Battalion—which whisked them to freedom across the bay. No POWs were killed in the raid, though several soldiers and Filipino guerillas were wounded, and two guerillas were killed. General Colin Powell recently stated: "I doubt that any airborne unit in the world will ever be able to rival the Los Baños prison raid. It is the textbook airborne operation for all ages and all armies."

CHAPTER EIGHT

Return to the U.S.A.
March–April 1945

GINNY, OUR FATHER, AND I LEFT for Leyte from Nichols Field in Manila sometime after March 13. A typhoon was brewing, and en route, our plane lost radio contact with the other planes in their formation. The others were ordered back, but our little plane flew on unaware, eventually facing poor visibility. The pilot became lost and had to fly low, over the water. With God's grace, we came to rainy Tacloban, Leyte (the island south of Luzon where MacArthur had landed months earlier), setting down on the corrugated metal runway.

The minute we stepped off the plane, American soldiers greeted us, offering candy. I had my first O'Henry bar there. We were piled into army trucks and taken to separate tent camps, the men into the jungle and the women and children onto the beach. We were given medical attention and inoculations, in preparation for entering the United States.

A big movie screen on the beach entertained everyone. The fronds of all the coconut trees had been shot off, proof of the intense battle that had taken place here. Our seats were the trunks of shot-down palm trees.

One of the soldiers invited Ginny, me, and others to take a joy ride on a landing barge. The sailor stopped the engine out in the water, joking that it had quit. It was fun, but we heard his superiors didn't think it was so amusing.

We were in Leyte for several days before being placed on a landing barge that took us to the U.S.S. *Admiral Capps*. There we sat for three days before the troop ship raised anchor and departed for the United States, around March 20. A more knowing friend told us that Gig Young, a Hollywood actor-turned-sailor, was onboard as well.

We slept on triple-deck bunks and enjoyed lots of food, including candy and oranges. I adored the apple butter. We were given crayons, called Payons, which could be used as normal crayons or dipped in water and used as watercolors. We watched movies, chatted with the soldiers, sailors, and marines, and played war. Soldiers made airplanes out of pieces of wood for us. Mass was held on deck, as we braced ourselves against the ship's plowing and swaying through the waves. We had to wear life belts at all times, and we practiced frequent abandon-ship drills. Lights were used with caution at night.

Sixty years after that trip, declassified records revealed that the State Department had taken the position that it was the responsibility of the civilians—those who, rather than being evacuated from the Philippines in the face of impending war, ended up being imprisoned for four years, 730 of them never to escape due to death from starvation in the prison camps, executions, and massacres—to pay their own way home. General MacArthur refused to accept such an arrangement, arguing with the State Department that the civilians, having lost everything during the Japanese occupation, were in no situation to pay their passage. This man, famed for his arrogance and miscalculations, stated that if the State Department was not willing to help out, then he would make the payment out of his own funds, and which Congress would later be obliged to reimburse. Realizing that he was serious, the State Department finally backed down.

The ship zigzagged in a convoy to Manus, in the Admiralty Islands (to make it a harder target for enemy subs). It was here that I discovered the piece of metal lodged inside the hinge of my right jaw, where I had been wounded by shrapnel (it was removed after we arrived in San Francisco). We stopped in Honolulu and then, eighteen days after leaving Leyte, docked in San Francisco at 7:48 a.m. on April 8.

Our approach to San Francisco was cold—coming from the tropics, we only had coats quickly sewn from army blankets (and I wore only a cotton red and white chenille beach cape, in an effort to look my best). But we wanted to be on deck when we went under the Golden Gate Bridge, so we spent our time going below to thaw out, then immediately running back up to make sure we didn't miss it. It was actually a relief when we went under it. I thought our ship was so tall that it might hit the bridge!

The Red Cross waited at the dock to greet us with warm drinks and doughnuts. Our mother's sister, Jerry Edwards, was there, too, with her friend and Red Cross member Mrs. William (Helen) Booth. Aunt Jerry had agreed to take Ginny and me into her care as we forged ahead into our new American life.

CHAPTER NINE

❖

Settling into American Life
1945-1947

AUNT JERRY, WHO TAUGHT AT THE SCHOOL of Public Health at UC Berkeley, took us to her home on Spruce Street in Berkeley. She was a good cook and made sure we ate a lot and were no longer malnourished. It was still wartime, so rationing was in place, with red tokens for meat and a book of stamps for other foods. Gas was also rationed — people had a sticker on their windshields that determined how much they were allotted.

On April 12, 1945, I had an appointment in San Francisco with Dr. Blackfield, the oral surgeon who had pulled the shrapnel out of my jaw; Roberta Gilbert, Aunt Jerry's friend and Mrs. Booth's sister, accompanied me. Walking on the streets toward his office, we learned that Roosevelt had died.

Soon, Ginny, our dad, and I headed east to Buffalo, New York, to visit Granny Blinzler. En route, the train was full of military personnel. One young soldier showed us how he could place a lighted cigarette on his little finger without hurting himself. Someone later said that he probably had some disease that affected the nerve endings and he couldn't feel pain (leprosy?).

It was a long trip, but I don't remember thinking that. Ginny and I shared a train seat and managed to sleep on it. In Buffalo, the local newspaper took a picture of us arriving (I still have a copy). Relatives greeted us warmly, and our visit ensued with a blur of nickel ice cream cones and baseball in the street and across people's backyards (no fences).

Then, we were off to New York City to visit Aunt Rosemary and our mother's other relatives. At Grand Central Terminal, Aunt Rosemary stood out with a red flower that she wore on her coat, since we hadn't met before. The mass of strangers surrounding and greeting us were introduced as aunts, uncles, and cousins.

We were in New York for V-E Day, May 8, 1945, but back in California for V-J day, August 14, 1945.

Dot, Curtis, and I have talked about how hard it was to transition back to normalcy after the war. Dot was in Long Island, New York, where it was cold, with grandparents she didn't know. She'd cry at night, missing her friends and the camaraderie that had developed within Santo Tomas, and her grandmother would tell her she shouldn't cry — she was safe. Curtis and his twin brother went back East to live with an uncle's family.

I attended sixth grade at Hillside Grammar School back in Berkeley that fall, but had a falling out with Aunt Jerry, who was pretty strict. So, set to start seventh grade at Garfield Junior High School, also in Berkeley, I went to live with Uncle Bob (my mother's and Jerry's brother) and Aunt Ollie and cousin Barbara Edwards. Their home was just a few blocks from Garfield, so that could have been part of the decision for me to move in with them. Here I finished seventh grade and continued with part of eighth grade.

I was prohibited from visiting Ginny at Aunt Jerry's without permission. One day I rode my bike to visit her, but Ginny couldn't let me in; we had to talk over the grape stake fence.

CHAPTER TEN

❖

Return to the Philippines
1947

IN DECEMBER 1947, GINNY AND I RETURNED to the Philippines to be with our father, who had gone back to working at the Balatoc Mine near Baguio. The ship stopped in Honolulu, where the grandmother of a classmate of Ginny's met us. She took us to a restaurant where we walked across stepping stones to reach our table perched over the water. Then she drove us around to see the Royal Hawaiian Hotel and the amazing views from the Pali. We also watched "The Yearling." She showed us a wonderful time in those 12 hours.

On board the ship, there was a circus troupe, and Ginny and I shared our room with a pinheaded woman—her head was very small. The woman in charge of the poor woman said, "Sit down or I'll box your ears!" I had never heard anyone talk like that to someone else. Two nuns with huge "flying" veils were also in the room. The ship had not yet been converted from a troop ship and still had bunks to sleep in.

A typhoon delayed our arrival in Manila, so we had to stay out at sea. It was Christmas, and to celebrate, some people decided to create a live tableau. I was selected to dress up as the Blessed Mother, wearing a borrowed blue bathrobe for my costume. Afterward there was a grand parade. I was changing when Ginny ran in and announced that I had won the grand prize. I hadn't even marched in the parade! My prize for best costume was a box of 20 Hershey bars.

Because of the typhoon and the accompanying swollen rivers and slides in the mountains, our father couldn't get down in time to greet us in Manila. He had someone from the Manila Benguet office take us through customs, and not long after, he was able to make it down.

We went to live at Acupan, part of Balatoc Mine, deep in the mountains near Baguio, where a portal brought out gold ore in mining carts. Someone caught a couple of cobras under our four-plex. And once, there was a big rockslide, but the rocks fell on either side of the house above ours; a huge boulder did land inside another house up above.

Brent International School opened for the first time after the war that year, and Ginny and I headed there for our studies. The question arose once again: What grade was I in? This time, I was boosted up half a year to ninth grade. There were 25 kids total, from kindergarten to twelfth grade; with five students total, my class was the largest.

The company provided an old station wagon to transport kids living at the mine to the school. It had open floorboards — the dust was something! The next year, with nine of us now, it was replaced by a new, smaller type bus that easily held us. One time there was a large iguana in the middle of the road, which the driver tried to hit to take home for dinner. Landslides sometimes blocked the road, so we couldn't get to school. Another time, Teddy, my dog, followed the school bus for some distance, so the driver let me pick him up. That was allowed only one time!

At some point, we moved to the Mill Site, in the central part of the mine. We lived with our father in a company-built, two-bedroom apartment in the upper right side of a four-plex. The layout was square; you entered into the living-dining room area, with the screened-in porch to the right. Our dad's bedroom was off the living room, and Ginny and I shared the back bedroom. A bathroom separated the bedrooms. Thriving in the tropical climate, orchids bloomed from bamboo tubes on the porch. A refrigerator had been purchased in Manila, but stoves were not yet available, so the mine made wood-burning ones. We had four burners on top and an oven.

The McLoughlins (sp?) lived across the hall from us. They brought us Mary, who was a dear, a Filipino from the lowlands. She was in charge of cooking and sometimes stayed with Ginny and me if our father went to town. Her quarters were separate, down by the mess hall. Frances helped out with the laundry and kept the house clean.

Teddy would meet the school bus every day. Dad rescued the

part-chow puppy while visiting a friend whose mother dog had been taken by the natives (who eat dogs). Ginny and I had been spending the weekend at the school, when he brought the puppy to us. We also had a black-and-white cat, Scotch.

One day I rescued some baby birds from native boys, who were going to use them as slingshot targets. I designed a cage, and our dad had someone at the mine make it, with the bottom part wood and the top part screen.

Our neighbors in the house to the right were the Burtons. Their son, Mike, Teddy, and I once went on a hike to explore in the mountains behind where we lived. Getting thirsty, we saw a native's hut and asked for *tubig* ("water"). Later on the hike, it started to rain, so we stood beneath big leaves to stay dry during the downpour.

There were three movie theaters in Baguio. One rainy day some friends and I were watching the movie "Bataan." We heard a large explosion outside and, thinking that a battle was brewing, people rushed out of the theater; it was only lightning that had struck a tree at the top of the main road.

We shopped at the Baguio market once a week. The market, arranged in rows of little straw booths, offered (and still does!) everything from strawberries to chayote to tapuey (Cordillera rice wine) to dressmaking and shoe resoling. Back then it had a place to buy dogs and chickens. I would go with one of the "girls" to stock up on produce. The U-Need grocery store provided the rest. Beef and pork had to be ordered once a month from Australia. We also ate chicken and fish. The chickens were live; attached to a stick in the yard, they didn't even have to be fed, with all of the bugs scurrying about.

My job was to write menus, but I had a hard time getting them together.

Some natives lived in huts above where we lived, and sometimes could be seen carrying a squealing pig tied to a pole and shouldered by two men.

In fall 1949, the Hukbalahaps (Huks), who were Communist guerrillas, were getting bolder. A bus carrying students from the American School in Manila had been ambushed. So our father felt it was safer for us to return to the United States for school. He was also concerned about getting us the proper background to enter college, so it seemed like the right decision.

When we left the Philippines in 1949, we gave Teddy to friends across the canyon. As we drove by their house, he sat on the porch as if he knew we were leaving him behind. Ginny gave the cat to Miss Davis, one of the teachers at Brent School, but were told he wandered away.

It was sad for us to say farewell to our dad on the dock in Manila. But, with six of ten passengers under the age of 20, Ginny and I had a wonderful trip to the United States on a Norwegian freighter, *The Triton*. We made several stops and could go ashore with stewardess passes, though we were told to take our meals on the ship as food was of short supply. We ate meals at one table with the captain — just like one family!

In Hong Kong we picked up a mother and her young son. At this time the communists were taking over China and the two were probably fleeing with the British. Her husband was a newspaper man, I think British. In Formosa (Taiwan), a pagoda was the only structure with some height. The shipping company loaned us an old station wagon and we visited a beach and some beautiful gardens in the mountains. Japan was occupied. In Yokohama we met a general who gave Marj (a friend who now lives in Livermore), her stepmother, Ginny, and me his chauffeur and car to take us into Tokyo one day. We visited the Ginza, and we got fresh milk. I ordered chocolate, but would have preferred white.

CHAPTER ELEVEN

❖

Back to the U.S.A. for Good
1949 and beyond

WE ARRIVED IN THE UNITED STATES and stayed a couple of days in the San Francisco Bay Area—me with Uncle Bob and Aunt Ollie (who now lived in Piedmont) and Ginny with a friend of our dad's in San Francisco. Aunt Jerry had us over for a barbecue; she still wasn't talking to me, but Roberta did.

We then flew off to the East Coast for school—Ginny to a "Visitation" school in Frederick, Maryland, and me at Georgetown Visitation Convent in Washington, D.C., which had been attended by our mother and her sisters. I completed two years of Visitation High School and two years of their junior college. Our cousin Gerry Hannan was also at Visitation at the time, and once she took me shopping for winter clothes. We still talk about the maroon suit she convinced me to buy.

My guardians until the age of 21 were Aunt Rosemary and Uncle Joe Hannan, who lived in Rye, New York. While at Visitation, I used to take the train to their home for Thanksgiving and Easter, and I stayed with them for a couple of summers. At first they lived in a two-plus-story house, where I slept in a room on the third level; and after cousins Gerry and Joe went to college they moved to a two-bedroom apartment—there, Aunt Rosemary and Uncle Joe slept in a hide-a-bed in the living room while the boys slept in one bedroom and I slept in the other with younger cousin Sue. Years later, Uncle Joe walked me down the aisle in Lady Chapel at St. Patrick's Cathedral.

Over Christmas vacation I would take the train to Granny Blinzler's in Buffalo to celebrate the holiday with she and Ginny, and I saw Ginny in Buffalo over summer vacation as well. Dad later left his job in the Philippines in 1953 and lived for a year in Buffalo, with Granny Blinzler, a brother, and possibly Aunt Rose (my great aunt). Ginny lived there at the time as well. He would interview for jobs and visit friends in different places. When I visited over that summer, he encouraged me to take driving lessons. He then moved to South Africa, where he remarried (to Cissy).

After graduating from Georgetown Visitation Preparatory High School on June 3, 1951, and Georgetown Visitation Junior College in June 1953, I went on to Northwestern University. Upon graduating from there, I thought about pursuing a career in advertising. I worked in that field for a bit, then tried teaching, which I loved. I moved to San Francisco in summer 1960, where I continued to teach intermediate grades. I earned a credential at San Francisco State night school and completed the degree with a correspondence course through UC Berkeley. While in San Francisco, I met Jim Noe, a lieutenant j.g. (supply officer) in the Navy who had spent time in Japan and the Philippines — but that's a whole other story!

Appendix

CHRONOLOGY

─────── ❖ ───────

August 27, 1932	Lee Blinzler and Kay Edwards elope to Medford, Oregon
June 18, 1933	Leanne Blinzler is born in San Francisco
July 1, 1934	Virginia Blinzler is born in Yreka
October 29 1936	The Blinzlers move to Marinduque, the Philippines
April 1937	Kay Blinzler dies
April 1937-1939	Leanne and Ginny live in Holy Ghost Convent & College, Manila
November 1939	Leanne and Ginny move to Baguio
December 1941	The Japanese attack Baguio and Clark Airfields (and Pearl Harbor)
December 1941	Leanne and Ginny flee to Manila
January 1942	Lee Blinzler is imprisoned in Santo Tomas Internment Camp. After a stint at an orphanage, the girls return to Holy Ghost Convent & College in Manila
March 10, 1944	Leanne and Ginny join Lee in STIC
February 3, 1945	MacArthur liberates the camp
April 1945	The Blinzlers return to the U.S.
December 1947	Leanne and Ginny return to the Philippines
Fall 1949	Leanne and Ginny move back to the U.S. for good

BIBLIOGRAPHY

Books

"Santo Tomas Internment Camp: Internews & Campus Health from January 24 to June 14, 1942," Relief for Americans in the Philippines, 1942.

Barnes-Payne, Georgia L., "Caught in the Crossfire: A Memoir," Polk, MO: Payne Prairie Publications, 1995.

Bloom, Greg, Michael Grosberg, Virginia Jealous, and Piers Kelly, "Lonely Planet Philippines, 10th ed.," Lonely Planet Publications, 2009.

Brechin, Gray, "Imperial San Francisco: Urban Power, Earthly Ruin," Berkeley and Los Angeles, California: University of California Press, 1999.

Carroll, Earl, "Santo Tomas Secrets," Archival Sources Taken From Original "Flash Back" to Internment 1942-1945, Reproduced and Distributed by Bay Area Civilian Ex-Prisoners of War Chapter of AXPOW," 1995.

Cogan, Frances B., "Captured: The Japanese Internment of American Civilians in the Philippines, 1941-1945," University of Georgia Press, 2000.

Day, Beth, "The Manila Hotel," self-published.

Flamm, Jerry, "Good Life in Hard Times, San Francisco's '20 and '30s," San Francisco: Chronicle Books, 1999.

Gudde, Erwin G., "California Gold Camps: A Geographical and Historical Dictionary of Camps, Towns, and Localities Where Gold Was Found and Mined; Wayside Stations and Trading Centers," University of California Press, 2009.

Hahn, Emily, "The Islands: America's Imperial Adventure in the Philippines," New York: Coward, McCann, & Geoghegan, 1981.

Hutton, Esther Robbins, "Sojourn: A Family Saga," Washington: Esfir Books, 1997.

Johansen, Bruce E., "So Far From Home: Manila's Santo Tomas

Internment Camp, 1942-1945," PBI Press, 1996.

Lucas, Celia, "Prisoners of Santo Tomas" Civilian Prisoners of the Japanese," Barnsley, South Yorkshire, England: Pen & Sword Paperback, 1996.

Norman, Elizabeth M., "We Band of Angels: The Untold Story of American Nurses Trapped on Bataan by the Japanese," Atria Books, 2000.

Payne, Georgia and Paul Schafer, eds., "Legacy of Captivity: Memoirs of American and British Civilians Interned in the Philippines," published for the 2002 Manila Liberation Reunion.

Ransom, Jay Ellis, "The Gold Hunters Field Book,"

Richards, Rand: "Historic San Francisco: A Concise History and Guide," San Francisco: Heritage House Publishers, 1991.

Sams, Margaret, "Forbidden Family: A Wartime Memoir of the Philippines 1941-1945," Madison, Wisconsin: University of Wisconsin Press, 1989.

Sides, Hampton, "Ghost Soldiers: The Forgotten Epic Story of World War II's Most Dramatic Mission," New York: Doubleday, 2001.

Wilson, Laurence Lee, "The Skyland of the Philippines," Baguio: Baguio Printing & Publishing Co., 1953.

Articles and Reports

"Gold Districts of California," Bulletin 193, California Division of Mines and Geology, Ferry Building, San Francisco, 1970.

"Report XIV of the State Mineralogist, California State Mining Bureau, Ferry Building, San Francisco," California State Printing Office, 1916.

LOS ANGELES TIMES STORY

A RETURN TO WARTIME PHILIPPINES

The writer's mother and other former prisoners confront memories as they visit World War II sites.

By Barbara A. Noe (Special to **The Times** *August 7, 2005*)

THE FLIGHT from San Francisco to Manila seemed endless, even though my mother had treated us to business class and its bedlike chairs, parade of meals and free-flowing champagne.

More than 60 years ago, my mother, Leanne Blinzler Noe, had traveled the same route by ship — taking 18 days instead of 13 hours. That realization was the first of many on a two-week tour last spring to my mother's childhood home in the Philippines, a place where she had run free across the Baguio Hills, learned to speak Tagalog, eaten the world's best mangos — and where she was a prisoner during World War II.

Her best friends in the prison camp, Dorothy Mullaney Brooks of Las Vegas and Connie Ford of Grass Valley, Calif., and a group of about 50 former soldiers and other Americans who had some connection to the Philippines during the war — had joined us on this trip. Because of them, this tour of battlefields and memorials on the 60th anniversary of their liberation became indelibly intertwined with their memories, creating for me a personal sketch of the war in the Philippines.

Before we left the U.S., Mom had said she was reluctant to return. "How was my childhood so different from others?" she had asked self-effacingly.

Manila before the war

FORESTS OF high-rises and smog-clouded, car-clogged streets dominate Manila, a sprawling metropolis with a population of 10.9 million. Group members said the capital looked nothing like the one they had known before the war. Then, Manila was called the Pearl of the Orient, an elegant city with broad, tree-shaded boulevards. That city was largely destroyed in World War II, changing the lives of my grandfather, mother and aunt.

On Jan. 2, 1942, the first Japanese soldiers arrived here. Thousands of civilians — executives of U.S. companies, ship passengers, diplomats, journalists and my grandfather, a mining engineer — were rounded up, told to pack food and clothes for three days, then taken to the University of Santo Tomas in the heart of Manila, where they were imprisoned for the rest of the war. My grandmother had died several years earlier, and my mother, who was then 9, and her younger sister, Ginny, lived safely for a time in a Manila boarding school run by German nuns. But in March 1944, they too were taken to Santo Tomas, each carrying a suitcase containing their sparse belongings.

For the modern-day tourist, Santo Tomas yields little about its days as a prison, aside from a brass plaque at the front entrance and a temporary exhibit. Many buildings have been added to the original layout, but the main edifice, a three-story Gothic structure where my mother, her family and friends were interned, was as Mom remembered it. She and Ginny lived in a classroom with women and other children; my grandfather was in another room with men. During the day, they could visit one another and eat meals together.

We climbed creaky mahogany stairs to the third floor, strolled down a window-lined hallway and found 55-A, their turquoise prison room, now re-numbered and again a classroom. I tried to imagine 26-odd cots, draped with mosquito nets, crammed wall to wall.

As my mother and her friends surveyed the desk-filled room, they struggled to hold back tears just as they had learned to do as girls all those years ago.

Dorothy, Connie and Mom reminisced about the 6 a.m. and 6 p.m. roll calls; of having to bow to Japanese sentries; of the unsatisfactory meals of watery lugao, or rice porridge; and the rare joy of finding a piece of water buffalo hide hidden inside the gruel.

Comforts were few, but one day my mother found a little rubber doll in the trash. "It was a little softened, sticky," she said, "but I don't know why someone threw it away. I took it and nurtured it, sewed clothes for it out of scraps."

Where it all started

THE WAR in the Philippines began Dec. 8, 1941, at Clark Air Base, about 40 miles northwest of Manila, the main base of the Army Air Forces in the Pacific. Japanese pilots, approaching the archipelago only eight hours after the attack on Pearl Harbor, found B-17 bombers parked wingtip to wingtip on the airfield.

Within minutes after Japan's attacks, the U.S. East Asian air forces were reduced by half, such an enormous blow that Gen. Douglas MacArthur was forced into defensive positions on Bataan and Corregidor just to the west.

Nothing at Clark today resembles its wartime appearance. Since its reversion to the Philippines in 1991, the base has been transformed into a civil aviation complex with industrial properties, a trade center and luxury hotels. But the Clark Museum provides a good historical retrospective with photos, dioramas and exhibits.

Perhaps its most telling artifact is out front, a burned, melted airplane part left from the Dec. 8 assault. Inside the museum, my mother pointed out Japanese wartime currency — they called it Mickey Mouse money — 75 Mickey Mouse pesos, or $35, could buy one duck egg, she said.

Tucked in one display was a black-and-white photograph of a Japanese kamikaze pilot. He looked like a kid, with an innocent smile. On a trip devoted to uncovering my mother's past, the photo also offered a window into the enemy side.

The world's first kamikaze pilot took off from nearby Mabalacat East Air Field in October 1944. Oddly, on this soil that suffered so much destruction at Japanese hands is a statue of a pilot standing tall and proud, paying tribute to the soldiers of the kamikaze, or "divine wind."

My mother said little about the statue, but I heard plenty of grumbling from former soldiers on our tour.

We then moved from Manila to the fortress island of Corregidor, an hour by ferry across Manila Bay. Open-air jeepneys loop around the 2-square-mile tropical island, taking visitors to World War II sites. The island remains almost as it was in early 1942, when for 27 days the Japanese starved, shelled and bombed the Allied defenders into surrendering on May 6, 1942.

Like many historic battlefields, Corregidor is exceedingly peaceful, its bombed-out, vine-tangled barracks, huge cannon and mortar batteries silent now. But you can't help but believe that ghosts swirl through the trees.

At the summit, where paratroopers retook the island in 1945, a sobering museum showcases Japanese bayonets, uniforms and photos of the American surrender. Nearby, a pavilion shades an eternal flame.

But Corregidor's pièce de résistance is a sound-and-light show in Malinta Tunnel, where MacArthur directed the war before being ordered to Australia, and military nurses, soldiers and Filipino scouts holed up, caring for the wounded. Flashes of light, recorded explosions and gunfire recount the story — sometimes too realistically.

From Corregidor, our group traveled north to the mosquito-infested Bataan Peninsula, site of one of the Pacific war's worst atrocities. After the Americans surrendered, the Japanese rounded up the defeated soldiers. They were weak and starving, but their captors gave them no food or water. Instead they force-marched 70,000 Americans and Filipinos 55 miles up the peninsula in the tropical heat. Thousands died on the way.

One in our group, Bob Wolfersberger, a spunky 86-year-old, survived. "It was a cattle drive out there," he said. "We were going up one side of the road, the Japanese coming down the other, lots of times swinging their clubs, hitting as many Americans as they could."

At the town of San Fernando at the head of the peninsula, the soldiers were packed into stifling, steamy train cars and shuttled to Capas, where they were forced to march seven more miles to Camp O'Donnell.

We walked only the last hot, dusty half a mile, arriving at the former prison's gates sheepishly thankful for the water fountain there. At the camp, now a memorial, monuments list the names of the Filipinos and Americans who died there. In a corner, a replica of the prisoners' barracks provides a hint of their misery.

"There was no food, no medicine," Wolfersberger said. "The prisoners were left to die in this concentration camp."

About 1,600 Americans died in the first 40 days at Camp O'Donnell. Survivors were transferred several months later to Cabanatuan, a former Army supply base about 25 miles east.

The camp at Cabanatuan is another memorial, with an altar-like monument flanked by Filipino and American flags. A wall has the names of dead soldiers.

A former Marine on our tour, Warren Elder, had been captured on Corregidor and imprisoned at Cabanatuan. At one point, he had been dragged out of the camp with four other soldiers expecting to be executed because "someone had done something," he said. But when the gun was fired, it just clicked; there was no ammunition. "They were just trying to scare us," Elder said in a shaky voice.

Prison camp rescues

IN 1942, THE AMERICANS began taking back the Pacific, winning such monumental battles as Coral Sea and Midway before finally coming ashore in the Philippines in October 1944. MacArthur began staging daring rescues at the prison camps, first at Cabanatuan on Jan. 31, 1945, then at Manila's Santo Tomas.

At 9 p.m. Feb. 3, 1945, an American tank — the *Georgia Peach* — crashed into the front gate. "Are you Americans?" a soldier shouted to the skinny prisoners who swarmed around the infantrymen. "Yes!" they yelled back.

After liberating the camp, the Army used Santo Tomas as its headquarters. One day, as Mom was in the plaza in front of the Main Building about to accept some chocolate from a soldier, a mortar shell exploded. Shrapnel hit her in the jaw; she still can open her mouth only partway. The soldier was killed.

My mother, aunt and grandfather — who weighed about 100 pounds at liberation — left the islands soon after, zigzagging across the Pacific to avoid detection of Japanese ships.

As our plane took off from Manila at the end of our tour, my mother gazed out the window into the night sky, lost in thought. For a few minutes the city's bright lights sparkled below, and then the blackness of the ocean fell. She absentmindedly reached out to touch my arm. When I think of her as a little child, surrounded by the horrors of war, of all the suffering that she and her fellow prisoners endured, I am awed — at their tenacity, at their will to survive.

Somehow, the flight back to the U.S. did not seem interminable.

LOS ANGELES TIMES STORY

❖

CALIFORNIA: YREKA A GOLD MINE OF NATURAL WONDERS

A mother and daughter's journey to Siskiyou County's Yreka digs up memories of a California gold rush amid a beautiful backwater.

By Barbara A. Noe (Special to **The Times** *December 2, 2012*)

YREKA, Calif. — Deep in Siskiyou County in far Northern California, high granite peaks and rocky streams have long incited gold miners, including my grandfather, who in the 1930s lived with his family — my grandmother, mother and aunt — in a two-room cabin near the Dewey gold mine southwest of Yreka.

My mother, who doesn't remember much about the area because she was 3 when they left, and I recently headed to this beautiful backwater to find out what we could about the gold mine where my grandfather worked and to bask in the region's simple charms.

Gold fever here dates back nearly as far as the famous Sierra Nevada gold rush. In March 1851, a mule-train packer named Abraham Thompson saw flakes of gold among the grass roots that his mules were eating near Black Gulch. Word got out, and by April, 2,000 miners were hoping to strike it rich at Thompson's Dry Diggings.

Within three months, tents and shanties had created a gold-rush boomtown. Several name changes occurred, but today the city is called Yreka. And though the region never garnered the fame of the Sierra Nevada and its gold rush, the amount of gold recovered here over the years is a mother lode itself: Millions of dollars' worth is said to have been mined in the area.

Miner Street, the heart of Yreka's historic district, is much quieter than in its heyday, a western fantasy of false-fronted buildings and balcony-shaded sidewalks, gentrified by restaurants, antiques shops and the Yreka Chamber of Commerce, where we start our quest for information.

"We're looking for the Dewey mine," I told the tourism rep. "We have a vague idea, but..." She pulled out a map and ran her fingers across the lines. "Hmm," she said. "If anyone would know, it's my son. He's a hunter and knows all those back roads." She called him and, sure enough, he said he knew exactly where it was: "Simply take the road out of Stewart Springs," he said through her. "But why would anyone go there? It's just a bunch of ruined buildings."

"If you're looking for gold," the woman continued, "you must visit the million-dollar gold display in the Siskiyou County Courthouse. It's the largest such display south of Alaska." At least it was a concrete plan, so off we went to the towering government building constructed in the mid-1850s.

Behind a wall of glass in the foyer (and in view of the building's security staff) lie piles of gold extracted in the county: huge nuggets, flakes and dust — all unpolished, rough and worth about $3 million. This is the same collection (minus some choice pieces that were stolen in the dark of night in February) that was displayed at the 1939 World's Fair in San Francisco to show the world the extent of riches found in Siskiyou County.

We strolled up West Miner Street, my mother taking a particular interest in No. 319, a historic building that now holds a scrapbooking shop. A sign indicated that the city's meat market, established in 1854, was housed here and in continuous operation until closing in 2009. My grandmother refers to the market in one of her letters to her family: In those Depression-era days, she bought a mere "0.08 cents worth of stew meat this morning and the man almost threw it at me."

At the tourism bureau's suggestion, we found the Yreka Third Street Inn, housed in a dollhouse-like 1897 Victorian; we stayed in the Rose Room, cozy with its hand-crocheted bedspreads and floral wallpaper. Innkeeper Hedley Cooper recommended a couple of places to eat on West Miner Street, each housed in a historic structure. We chose the casual Brickhouse pizzeria, where we enjoyed vegetarian pizza and a simple green salad. (The homemade vinaigrette alone is worth coming back for.)

The next morning, hoping to find more information, my mother and I headed to the small Siskiyou County Museum, also on Miner Street, with impressive displays of the region through the ages. On a wall, I discovered a sepia-toned photo of the Dewey mine, with a row of men hanging out in front of its wooden shaft. The photo was dated before my grandfather's time, but this must have been the mine where he worked.

The receptionist was kind enough to indulge our curiosity, and she pored over maps and books that she pulled from the back room, to no avail. Dewey mine, she said, had been one of the biggest, but it closed in 1907.

"Maybe my father was hired to try to reopen it," my mother said. We head south and west out of Yreka on California Highway 3, through long, golden Scott Valley with its cows, horses and backdrop of granite (gold-filled) peaks. We passed through Fort Jones, named after a military outpost established there in 1852.

At the nearby Forest Service office, we told a ranger about our quest. He studied several Forest Service maps but even he seemed a bit perplexed about our mine. Finally, he pinpointed it somewhere east of Mountain House Creek and north of China Mountain, and noted a road leading south off Gazelle-Callahan Road to reach it.

"What's the road like?" I asked.

"Dirt," he says. "You'll need an SUV to get there."

Continuing south on Highway 3, we came to Etna, where my grandparents had a post-office box. I'll bet the little town hasn't changed much since they were here; it's essentially one street with western facades, the highlight being Scott Valley Drug, in business since 1902. The drugstore has an old-fashioned walk-in safe to hold the gold nuggets that were exchanged for goods and an 1800s soda fountain with a pine back bar.

We had lunch at the Etna Brewing Co., which served delicious salads, soups and sandwiches — and locally brewed beer — on its sunny patio. We both had the delicious pub chili, the secret of which is Old Grind Porter (a dark-brown beer) added to the spicy sauce. Afterward, we headed along the Scott River, noticing rock pilings left from mining days. We didn't spot any modern miners, though gold panners and dredgers still forage the area. We passed through the ghost town of Callahan, its buildings looking as though a slight breeze could tip them over.

We veered onto Gazelle-Callahan Road, climbing, twisting and turning through gorgeous pine-forested mountains. In the distance, jagged, gun-gray peaks march in rows.

I studied the map and saw that based on what the Forest Service ranger told us, the turnoff to the mine occurred after a huge U curve in the road. It looked as though we were driving along such a U, and just as I glanced to the right and saw a dirt lane winding into the forest, the road crested and dropped down the other side of the mountain in a series of precarious switchbacks.

"I think that's the road to the mine!" I said.

But my mother was driving too fast, and there are no turn-arounds.

Maybe she was concerned about getting stuck on a rutted dirt road — or perhaps she didn't want to disturb sleeping ghosts, but there was no turning back.

As we zoomed down the mountain at a faster speed than my grandparents could ever have imagined in their Depression-era Ford, I knew one thing for sure: The region is worth a visit just for its gold mine of natural splendors.

INDEX

Bold page numbers indicate illustrations.

B
Bataan 30, 32, 34, 35, 54, 77
Bataan Death March 35
Baguio xi, 16, 19, 21–28, 30, **43, 51,** 75, 76, 77
Baguio Country Club 22, 23
Balatoc Mine 23, 75
Battle of Manila xi, 40, **48,** 64, 66
Battlin' Basic 61, 64
Bohen, Geraldine (Gran Edwards) 1
Brent School 24, 76, 78
Brereton, Maj. Gen. Lewis 26

C
Cavite 27
Clark Airfield 26, 91
Corregidor 30, 32, 34, 36, 54, 67

D
Del Mundo, Dr. Fay 35
Dewey Mine xi, 1, 5, 6, 9, 10, **41**

E
Edwards, Case 1
Edwards, Geraldine (Jerry) 1, 2, 3, 4, 7, 73, 74, 79
Edwards, Aunt Rosemary (Hannan) 1, 4, 7, 8, 9, 13, 14, 15, 16, 73, 79
Elks Club ii, 30, 32
Eisenhower, Maj. Gen. Dwight 26

F
54th Evacuation Hospital 65
Far East Air Force 26, 27
First Cavalry 59, 60, 61

G
Gazelle, Calif. 3, 5, 6, 8, 10
Guytingco, Lt. Diosdado 58-59

H
Holy Ghost College & Convent xi, 16, 18, 29, 33, 34, 35, **51**
Holy Ghost Hill 19, 21, 23, 28, **43**
Hukbalahaps 77
Hull, Cordel 25

I
Iba Airfield 27, 54, 55, 66, 69, 70

L
Landon, Alf 14
Leyte 54, 55, 66, 69, 70
Liberation **47, 49,** 56, 57, 59–68
Lingayen Gulf 27, 30, 57, 59

Los Baños 67–68
Luzon Island xi, 13, 19, 21, 27, 30, 54, 57, 59, 60, 64

M

MacArthur, General Douglas xi, xii, 23, 24, 26, 27, 30, 31, 32, 34, 36, 54, 55, 59, 64, 65, 67, 70
Manila x, xi, 13–19, 21, 24, 25, 29–32, 33, 36, 37, 38, 39, 40, **44**, 59, 60, 64, 66, 67, 69, 75, 76, 77, 78
Marinduque 13-19
Mindinao 27

N

Nichols Field 27, 69

Q

Quezon, President Manuel 24, 26

R

Rainbow-5 (war plan) 24, 26, 30
Roosevelt, Franklin D. 14, 24, 27, 30, 32, 34, 73

S

St. Anthony's Convent 29
Santo Tomas Internment Camp (STIC) 32, 35, 36, 37–59, **45, 46, 47, 52,** 64 67, 68
Sayre, Francis B. 25
Siskiyou County, California xii, 1-11

U

University of Santo Tomas 32, 35, 37–40, 53-57
U.S.S. *Admiral Capps* 69

W

War Plan Orange 24, 30

Y

Yreka, California 1–11

ILLUSTRATIONS CREDITS

All illustrations courtesy of Leanne B. Noe except the following:

ix map: NordNordWest; ix inset: Lambanog; x map: public domain; 45 bottom: U.S. Army Signal Corps; 46 top: National Archives; 46 middle: Japanese propaganda photo; 46 bottom: Carl Mydans, Life Images; 47: Carl Mydans, Life Images; 48 top: John T. Pilot/U.S. Air Force; 48 bottom: John T. Pilot/U.S. Air Force; 51 top and middle: Barbara A. Noe; 51 bottom: from Lee's Christmas card; 52 all: Barbara A. Noe.

ACKNOWLEDGMENTS

To my daughter, Barbara Noe, whose talents, skills, interest, diligence, patience, and energy birthed this story; the adventurous spirit of Lee and Kay Blinzler, our parents, which provided the opportunities for this story of our lives; and Curtis Brooks, who survived the prison camp with us and later became a friend and good source of memories.

www.ingramcontent.com/pod-product-compliance
Lightning Source LLC
Chambersburg PA
CBHW060202050426
42446CB00013B/2957